IN HIS SPIRIT

IN HIS SPIRIT

A Guide to Today's Spirituality

Richard J. Hauser, S.J.

 PAULIST PRESS ● New York/Mahwah, N.J.

Other books by Richard J. Hauser, S.J.
published by Paulist Press

FINDING GOD IN TROUBLED TIMES
MOVING IN THE SPIRIT

The Publisher gratefully acknowledges the use of the following materials:
Excerpt from *New Seeds of Contemplation* by Thomas Merton, © 1961 by New Directions Publishing Corporation. Used by permission.
Excerpt from *The Climate of Monastic Prayer* by Thomas Merton, © 1969 by the Merton Legacy Trust. Published by Cistercian Publications Inc., Kalamazoo, Michigan. Used with permission.
Excerpt(s) from *The Jerusalem Bible,* copyright © 1966 by Darton, Longman & Todd, Ltd., and Doubleday & Company, Inc. Used by permission of the publisher.

Library of Congress
Catalog Card Number: 81-83187

ISBN: 0-8091-2421-1

Published by Paulist Press
997 Macarthur Boulevard
Mahwah, New Jersey 07430

www.paulistpress.com

Printed and bound in the
United States of America

CONTENTS

Acknowledgements

I am indebted to *Review for Religious* for permission to use matter in the final four chapters of this book which originally appeared in the *Review*. I am also indebted to Sr. Mary Lenz, O.S.F., Mrs. Mary Lou Kuhlman, and Mrs. Jan Gines for their work on the manuscript. I am grateful to Sr. Gertrude Ann Mertens, O.S.F., Sr. Perpetua Elliott, O.S.M., and the Poor Clare Sisters of Omaha for their spiritual support. Finally, I am grateful to Fr. Don Doll, S.J., and Mrs. Mary Jo Nakashima for their immense personal support.

Richard J. Hauser, S.J.
Creighton University
Omaha, Nebraska

To
My mother and father
for everything

INTRODUCTION

For the past ten years I have been in dialogue with groups about various topics in Christian spirituality. These groups have been remarkably diversified, including undergraduate college students, adult lay Christians, Catholic sisters and priests, Protestant ministers, and graduate students in the field of Christian spirituality. This book is in large measure a combination of my own personal research and experiences held against and conditioned by the insights and experiences of each of these groups. The focus of my presentations has been personal prayer, since this is my chief personal and professional interest. But the more I presented matter on prayer, the more convinced I became that prayer was impossible to discuss adequately apart from the entire spiritual life. Consequently, my presentations began to include topics on sin and grace, the Holy Spirit, discernment of spirits, religion and personality, and asceticism. This book pulls together the insights in each of these areas that have been most meaningful to my students. It is a general introduction to the Christian spiritual life with a particular emphasis on personal prayer.

I have titled the book, *In His Spirit: A Guide to Today's Spirituality*. The Holy Spirit is the organizing motif of each chapter. In giving presentations on the spiritual life I discovered that most of our misunderstandings flowed from lack of appreciation of the role of the Spirit; we simply do not take seriously the role of the Spirit whom Jesus sent to take his place among us and be our sanctifier. The book blends a theoretical understanding of the Spirit flowing from Scripture and contemporary theology with a practical application of this theory to daily life. Chapter I presents two models of spirituality, one respecting the role of the Spirit, the other not. Chapter II puts the role of the Spirit in the widest context by surveying the New Testament message on the practical effects of the Spirit in Christian life. Chapter III narrows the context by presenting a theology of prayer centered on the role of the Spirit. Chapter IV presents a general method for improving prayer by greater respect for the role of the Spirit. Chapter V gives principles with practical application for living daily life in tune with the Spirit. Chapter VI focuses on the unity of the two main elements of the spiritual life, prayer and service, stemming from their rootedness in the Spirit of Christ. I should note also that the text contains many quotations from Thomas Merton since he has been my primary guide in understanding contemporary spirituality.

I have opted to write the book in an informal manner, generally using the first person. Presentations on the spiritual life seem to gain credibility to the extent they can be illustrated by personal examples. Spiritual theology is a reflection on the experience of living the Gospel in the Christian community. All of us, as members of the community, are in touch with this experience to one degree or another. I learned very early that if I wanted my theoretical insights to be taken seriously, I had to come up with examples from my own experiences of living the Christian life. The text, then, is a blend of my insights illustrated by personal experience. I have learned, further, that the insights I present are not fully grasped by my students until they are able to hold them against their own experience of living the Gospel. Only at this point do they move to the fullest possible comprehension. To facilitate this process I have included reflection questions at the end of each chapter. These questions have a focus quite different from the usual end-of-chapter questions. Typical discussion questions aim at increasing comprehension by stimulating dialogue on the ideas presented. These questions aim at increasing comprehension by application of the matter presented to one's own experience. Hence I have self-consciously called these "reflection" questions rather than "discussion" questions. There is, of course, nothing wrong with discussing the ideas I have presented. However, this discussion will not be as profitable in grasping the ideas as will relating them to personal experience. Only at this point will the ideas be understood and able to be discussed accurately, if the reader wishes.

For the most effective use of this book, I would suggest a threefold process. The first stage is a quiet and reflective reading of each chapter aimed at an accurate understanding of the ideas presented. The second stage is applying the insights to one's own experience by using the reflection questions. The third and final stage is sharing responses to these questions in a small group or with another person. Sharing personal application has two great benefits. First, by articulating our own experiences we become much more in tune with them, and second, by listening to others articulate theirs we become more aware of similar personal experiences. It is a humbling thing for a teacher to admit, but in the area of spirituality the best learning goes on when a student understands the matter in light of personal experience and has the courage to share this understanding with the group. I have found that it is only at this point that many of the group finally "get it."

The focus of this book is the Holy Spirit, the Spirit that Jesus sent to continue his work among us till the end of time. It could be objected that not enough attention is given to Christ himself. It should always be remembered that the Spirit we receive is the same Spirit that moved Jesus. As we open ourselves more and more to the influence of this Spirit, we come closer to Jesus and ever more like him. We cannot forget Jesus if we live in his Spirit.

I TWO MODELS OF SPIRITUALITY

At the heart of an understanding of Christian spirituality is an adequate understanding of the self. Spirituality is our effort with grace to become what we have been created by the Lord to be; we must grasp who we truly are in order to know what we are to become. Many of us have an inadequate understanding of who we are; so we also have an inadequate understanding of spirituality. I find it very helpful to begin an understanding of spirituality by contrasting the view of the self presented in Scripture with the view of the self held by most of us Westerners and to draw out the implications for Christian spirituality flowing from each view, I am calling the scriptural model of the self, the *self-in-God*, and the Western model of the self, the *self-outside-God*. I will begin by describing the two views of the self with their approaches to spirituality. I will then review briefly two psychological models of the self for their compatibility with the scriptural model. It goes without saying that the human person is a very complex phenomenon. In no way am I attempting to present a complete view of the person. I will be discussing but one aspect of the person, the aspect which I believe holds the key for best illuminating the nature of Christian spirituality.

Scriptural Model of the Person: The Self-in-God

The indispensable starting point for understanding Christian spirituality is an acceptance of the view of person presented in the New Testament. The New Testament is emphatic in stressing the fact that human nature is different because of the resurrection of Jesus. The difference is the result of the sending of the Holy Spirit by

Jesus and the Spirit's new presence in the world in those believing in Jesus. Peter's first sermon on Pentecost sums this up:

> "You must repent," Peter answered, "and every one of you must be baptized in the name of Jesus Christ for the forgiveness of your sins, and you will receive the gift of the Holy Spirit" (Acts 2:38).[1]

Paul emphasized this new reality in a particularly effective way for his Jewish Christians. Before Jesus and the sending of the Spirit, the primary presence of the Lord on earth was in the revered temple of Jerusalem. But now no more:

> Didn't you realize that you were God's temple and that the Spirit of God was living among you? If anybody would destroy the temple of God, God will destroy him, because the temple of God is sacred; and you are that temple (1 Cor. 3:16–17).

John's metaphor of the vine and the branches and Paul's of the body of Christ are only two of the more dramatic ways the New Testament uses to emphasize this new presence of God in his people.

But the Scripture message does not simply point out the fact of a new presence of God in believers; it further insists that this Spirit is continually active and powerful in their lives. The newly born Christian community is now primarily characterized by activities that flow from the presence of the Spirit. These effects are nowhere more obvious than in the Acts of the Apostles. We need only recall the difference in the first disciples before and after the reception of the Spirit at Pentecost to see the effect the Spirit had on them. Jesus himself recognized that it would be necessary for the Spirit to come in order for his disciples to begin their mission.

> "...but you will receive power when the Holy Spirit comes on you, and then you will be my witnesses not only in Jerusalem but throughout Judaea and Samaria, and indeed to the ends of the earth" (Acts 1:8).

For Paul this new life was so significant that he did not hesitate to speak of it in terms of a new creation. He contrasts the creation in

Christ and the creation in Adam: "And for anyone who is in Christ, there is a new creation; the old creation has gone, and now the new one is here" (2 Cor. 5:17). Paul's witness is particularly compelling because he knew what it was to live without Christ and the new power that comes with belief. It was only in Christ that Paul personally found the power to be freed from his sinful tendencies and to live according to his spiritual self.

> In fact, this seems to be the rule, that every single time I want to do good it is something evil that comes to hand. In my inmost self I dearly love God's law, but I can see that my body follows a different law that battles against the law which my reason dictates. This is what makes me a prisoner of that law of sin which lives inside my body. What a wretched man I am! Who will rescue me from this body doomed to death? Thanks be to God through Jesus Christ our Lord (Rom. 7:21–25).

Paul saw the entire world as mired in sin before Christ came. But he assured the Romans to whom he was writing that this same power which has been triumphant in him personally was also stronger than the power of sin in the world and could be triumphant in the world, no matter how sinful it was previously.

> . . . but however great the number of sins committed, grace was even greater; and so, just as sin reigned wherever there was death, so grace will reign to bring eternal life thanks to the righteousness that comes through Jesus Christ our Lord (Rom. 5:20–21).

And for Paul the presence of the Spirit had an even greater implication. As a good Jew he had formerly been under the law and striven to fulfill all its prescriptions; the effort was difficult and unsuccessful and Paul frequently calls himself a slave to the law. The law imposed an obligation but it did not give the power to fulfill the obligation. However, the Spirit had freed him from the law. Paul's life was now directed not at fulfilling external prescriptions of a written law but at responding to the internal directions of the Spirit.

Since this law was written within him, it gave the power to fulfill what it directed. It would always be triumphant over the unspiritual self.

> So then, my brothers, there is no necessity for us to obey our unspiritual selves or to live unspiritual lives. If you do live in that way, you are doomed to die; but if by the Spirit you put an end to the misdeeds of the body, you will live (Rom. 8:5–6).

God's Spirit had joined our spirit and would now direct our lives.

Any presentation of the scriptural view of the person that presented us as having only tendencies toward good flowing from the presence of the Holy Spirit is obviously inadequate. The New Testament stresses that we are divided beings, also possessing tendencies toward evil. We continually experience pressures from within ourselves as well as from our external environment moving us away from the inclinations of the Spirit. But the clear message of Scripture is that we need not be controlled by these inclinations. The presence of the Spirit does not take away the inclinations—it surely did not for Paul!—but it does give us power not to be controlled by them; grace is stronger than sin. Christ, our redeemer, frees us from the power of sin.

In order to fully understand the New Testament view of the person, it is important to understand the meaning of grace. Paul uses the term often; it means for him everything God has given us in Jesus Christ. The Holy Spirit, then, is really the completion of what God has given us in Jesus. Let us consider grace as the power given us through the presence of the Spirit to enter into a deeper relationship with Christ and so become more like him. Our relationship to Christ is similar to human relationships: we are different because of our relationships; in some sense we become like those people we love. It is the same with Jesus. As the Spirit draws us into a deeper relationship with Jesus, we become more like him. But there is an important difference, a difference that is central to an adequate understanding of Christian spirituality. In this relationship Christ is always the initiator; his role is always primary. We can go to him only because he first draws us to himself. Any movement toward Christ, any movement toward good, occurs because he sends his help, his Spirit. It goes without saying that we have a crucial role in keeping ourselves open to the Lord as he extends his initiative—for we are free to ignore his promptings and act contrary to them—but this should not dilute the fact that we move toward the Lord and toward good because he enables us to move.

The scriptural model of the person insists that the Holy Spirit is present in us, continually active in us and continually extending initiative moving us away from evil toward good. This model has great implications for Christian spirituality. Spirituality is our effort with grace to become who we truly are. The deepest level of our being is spiritual. This is the level of our freedom and love. Here we are free to move out in love toward God and others or to live a self-centered existence. It is at this level that the Spirit of God is united with the human spirit; at this level God's Spirit joins our spirit. To be true to our deepest nature we Christians have the immense task of becoming aware of the movements of the Spirit and responding to them at all times, during our work, our recreation, our prayer. A constellation of attitudes toward spirituality flows from this New Testament model of the self. It is helpful to enumerate the more important ones: emphasis is placed on internal attitudes rather than external actions; the Spirit initiates all good desires and we listen and respond; the focus is on love for God and others rather than on any reward for the self; emphasis is on union and love in this life rather than concern about the next life. For brevity, I am calling the scriptural model of the person the self-in-God model.

Western Model of the Person: The Self-Outside-God

The Western model of the person is quite different from the scriptural model. It is usually not explicitly articulated, but its assumptions affect our understanding and living of the Christian life. I am presenting it here to highlight the scriptural model by contrast. If the New Testament model can be summarized as the self-in-God model, the Western model can be summarized as the self-outside-God model. The difference in prepositions is crucial. In the Western model the existence of God is never disputed, but God is seen residing primarily in heaven, outside the self: "God's in his heaven; all's right with the world." The transcendence of God is so stressed that there is little or no acknowledgement of God's immanence. Here I must be careful not to exaggerate, for the Western model does acknowledge in a vague intellectual way the presence of God in the person— baptism confers sanctifying grace, and the Eucharist and good actions increase that grace—but this presence of God is never really taken seriously; it has no practical effect on actions. In this model the person is a complexus of body, mind, and spirit—but the spirit is seen as human decision-making faculty not in touch with the Holy Spirit. In this model, God's Spirit has not joined our spirit; the model is, therefore, contrary to Scripture.

And this model also effects a distinctive approach to spirituality. Since the Spirit is not present in the person, all good desires and actions must originate from natural capacities. Persons operating under this model make every effort to please God by the correct use of all their natural capacities. Since the person is understood to be a complexus of only natural operations, this is the logical conclusion regarding spirituality. Persons operating under the assumptions of the Western model—and this includes all of us at times—see all their good intentions and actions as flowing solely from their own desires to please God. They do not see the Holy Spirit as having any role. In my experience this view of the self and its approach to spirituality is the dominant model for most Westerners and is operative in all of us at times.

Here again a footnote on the theology of grace is important, for those of us operating under the Western model have a vastly different theology of grace. Grace is the reward given by God to the person for good deeds. It exists and is stored up in a heavenly treasury outside the individual; it is not an internal power flowing from the presence of the Spirit of Christ. As the person conscientiously strives to love and serve God, this heavenly treasure is increased; as it increases the person becomes more pleasing to God. In short, through efforts flowing only from personal initiative the individual does good works of prayer and service all day long, and God in turn rewards these efforts with an increase of grace. The accompanying diagram illustrates the two models presented.

The Western model of the person is clearly incompatible with

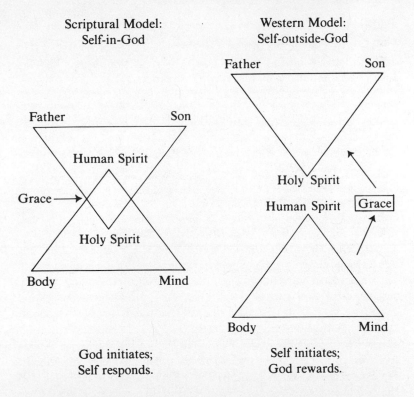

Scriptural Model:
Self-in-God

Western Model:
Self-outside-God

God initiates;
Self responds.

Self initiates;
God rewards.

the scriptural model. In addition, its approach to Christian spirituality is also at odds with the New Testament. A constellation of attitudes surrounds this spirituality quite different from the scriptural model: external deeds are more important than internal motivation; the self is the initiator of all good deeds and God is the rewarder; reward and punishment for deeds are often the primary motivation rather than love for God and others; guarantees of eternal life are often more important than union and love of God in this life. In my experience, the assumptions buried in the Western model of the person are operative in all of us at some times, even though they are usually not consciously articulated. Growth in the understanding of the true nature of Christian spirituality comes only after these assumptions are recognized and held against the New Testament approach to spirituality.

Comparison of Models

It is easy to see that the two models presented have vastly different attitudes to spirituality. At the risk of repetition, it may be helpful to juxtapose the main tenets of these models:

Scriptural Model	*Western Model*
God initiates and person responds	Person initiates and God rewards
Grace is transformation of the total person into the likeness of Christ by the freely given gift of the Holy Spirit	Grace is treasury of merit stored up in heaven and earned by good deeds
Focus is on love of God and others now	Focus is on reward for self now or in heaven after death
Emphasis is on internal attitudes and continual awareness of the Spirit's movements	Emphasis is on sporadically performed external deeds

To gain the most from this analysis it is important to be very concrete. The practical question is: Do I adequately acknowledge the Spirit's role in the good actions I perform every day, or do I attribute them only to my own initiative and hard work? The scriptural model insists that if the action was good, the Spirit was present from the beginning to the end. Since I am a teacher of theology it is most important for me to acknowledge God's role in this area. Do I see the desire in me to teach well for the love of God and others as coming from the Spirit? Do I recognize that the strength and insight to carry out the good desire well are also infused by the Spirit? At the end of the day, do I adequately acknowledge God's role in my successes and give God appropriate thanks? In addition to my teaching, I must do the same review for my counseling, my committee work at the university, my writing, my prayer, my helping others in any way throughout the day. I have allowed grace to be present and operative in myself to the extent that I have tried to do my daily service for the love of God and others. To this extent the Spirit of life in Christ Jesus our Lord has been dominant over the pressures on me not to serve with love. To the extent that I have not served in love, I humbly admit my faults and ask for a greater increase of grace to transform these areas. My reward for living in the Spirit is the habitual peace and joy I experience.

It cannot be stressed enough that the self-outside-God approach to spirituality is a distortion of the New Testament. It attributes to the self what in truth flows from the Spirit. In it God is not permitted to be God; grace is not grace. The saddest fact of all is that the conscientious person living under the Western model will never truly appreciate the presence and power of God in daily life. Erroneously attributing to the self what clearly is of God, the person will never understand the all-pervasiveness of God's love and activity.

Psychological Models and Trust of the Self

The key to understanding Christian spirituality is the acceptance of the scriptural model of the self and all the implications it contains. There is one corollary of this model that in my experience is not adequately recognized: trust of the self. If God's Spirit has truly joined our spirit, then we have every reason to trust the deepest inner movements of our natures. This trust becomes a key for all spirituality. The goal of Christian spirituality is to recognize and respond to the continual interior movements of the Spirit, for the Spirit will always lead us toward greater union with Christ and greater love and service of God and others. In my experience, many of us are able to intellectually accept the self-in-God approach to spirituality, but we are not able to trust the inner movements of the Holy Spirit implied in this approach. We have a predominantly distrustful attitude toward human nature, and this conditions our approach to spirituality. Just as it is necessary to expose the Western model of spirituality in ourselves, so it is also necessary to expose the predominantly distrustful attitude to the self, if it does exist in us. I will present two models of human nature taken from psychological theories of personality that reflect contrasting views of human nature, the first trustful of the self and the second distrustful. I don't believe that most of us consciously articulate a psychology of human nature and its trustworthiness, but I believe each of us has implicit attitudes toward the subject. My own growth in the understanding and practice of spirituality was greatly helped by my uncovering an essentially very distrustful attitude toward my deepest self.

Perhaps a short note should be added on the criteria to be used for assessing the adequacy of personality models from psychology. For believers revelation is the ultimate norm of truth. This is not to say that a person must be a Christian to do valid empirical science, such as psychology, but a Christian approach does insist that the conclusions of empirical science be compatible with the basic facts of revelation. There can be no contradiction between truth arrived at from empirical science and Christian revelation. Where one does exist, it is because science is inadequate or because the theological explanation of revelation is inadequate. And history witnesses to the frequent occurrence of both! Again we must recall that the human personality is an immensely complex phenomenon and that no personality theory has gained general acceptance as reflecting this phenomenon adequately. Each theory seems to explain one particular aspect of human nature better perhaps than another. None explain well the psychological dynamics of the total person. I have chosen two theories to be examined under one aspect only—namely, how well do they reflect the positive internal growth forces that are the result of the presence of the Holy Spirit? If the theory does not allow for an essentially positive thrust within the human person which can be trusted to lead the person toward good, I am judging it to be inadequate because it is incompatible with revelation.

Trusting the Self: Spirituality as Transformation

For the Christian, there are three keys for adequately understanding the human person: creation, sin, and redemption. The theology of creation insists that God created us in his own image, with a dynamic orientation toward loving and serving him in all. From the beginning we shared in the essential goodness of all of God's creation. But God also created us free. The theology of sin insists that from the very beginning human beings abused this freedom, yielding to internal and external pressures to serve themselves only and ignore his commands. Finally, the theology of redemption insists that God sent the Son into the world to reinforce the basic goodness of our creation and to give us new strength to overcome our evil tendencies and use our freedom for loving and serving God in all. The theology of redemption emphasizes that the power of the grace of Christ in us is stronger than the power of sin in us; consequently Christ has freed us from sin. We have seen how this truth of freedom from sin is expressed in Paul. The conclusion for us is that we can now trust our deepest self. At our center dwells the Holy Spirit of God reinforcing the dynamic goodness of our creation and enabling us to transform our evil inclinations. Christian spirituality becomes our effort with grace to put more and more of our life under the dominance of the Spirit. It is very helpful to have a theory of personality that acknowledges the basic positive thrust of our natures toward good and that sees the growth forces within us as more powerful than the destructive forces.

One such personality model is the self-actualization theory of Abraham Maslow. This model has been very important for me. Until I became acquainted with it, I had been implicitly embracing a very negative model of myself. I read about the Spirit and the Spirit's power, but I was never really able to acknowledge it because I believed human beings, especially myself, were dominated by evil and coping as well as they could. I had not truly grasped the fact that the grace of Christ in us, transforming our natures created good by the Lord, is stronger than the power of evil in us. Here a caution is in order. Maslow is not a Christian, nor even a believer in God. He does not present his theories in theological terms; he goes no further than stating his conclusions in the language of psychology. He himself reacted strongly to the suggestions that there is a power outside the self that reinforces goodness within the self. In this sense he is at odds with Christian revelation, since he denies God and his immanence in human beings. Yet there is a basic dynamism to his theory that I find very compatible with revelation. As a Christian viewing his theory with the eyes of faith, I can see the power of the Spirit working within the psychological model he presents, bringing the person to wholeness by following the deepest tendencies of the self. I am led by Maslow to an attitude of basic trust of my deepest self. For me this was crucial in developing a better understanding of Christian spirituality.

A quote from the early writing of Maslow presents the three pillars of his theory: (1) human nature contains a structured inner essence; (2) growth is the result of trusting and developing this inner nature; (3) sickness is the result of violating this nature.

> Now let me try to present briefly and at first dogmatically the essence of this newly developing conception of the psychologically healthy man. First of all and most important of all is the strong belief that man has an essential nature of his own, some skeleton of psychological structure that may be treated and discussed analogously with his physical structure, that he has some needs, capacities, and tendencies that are part genetically based, some of which are characteristics of the whole human species, cutting across all cultural lines, and some of which are unique to the individual.
>
> Second, there is involved the conception that full health and normal and desirable development consist in actualizing this nature, in fulfilling these potentialities, and in developing into maturity along these lines that his hidden, covert, dimly seen essential nature dictates, growing from within rather than being shaped from without.
>
> Third, it is now seen clearly that most psychopathology results from the denial or the frustration or the twisting of man's essential nature. By this concept what is good? Anything that conduces to this desirable development in the direction of actualization of the inner nature of man. What is bad or abnormal? Anything that frustrates or blocks or denies the essential nature of man.[2]

For Maslow, this essential nature is an hierarchically arranged order of needs inherent in our organic makeup, ranging from the need for food at the lowest level to the need for an ultimate value at the highest level. The following are the four basic needs common to all persons: physiological, security, love and belongingness, respect. Maslow calls these *basic needs* because they must all be fulfilled to some degree before the person can be motivated predominantly by the next higher set of needs—which also emerge in hierarchical order—that Maslow calls *being needs*. These are: the need to develop one's own unique talents and potentialities (self-actualization need), the need to know and understand the meaning of life better (curiosity need), and the need for an ultimate value toward which to orientate all life. Growth results from trusting this inner nature and listening and responding to the promptings of each level of need as it arises. Lack of growth comes from ignoring the promptings toward a higher level of need fulfillment and remaining on the lower level. One's inner nature will direct the person up the entire hierarchy of needs. Only the person whose entire life is orientated toward serving an ultimate value, such as truth, justice, and beauty, is mature and fully developed in Maslow's schema.

There are elements of Maslow's theory of human nature that are incompatible with Scripture. For me these elements are outweighed by his basic positive approach of trusting our inner nature. I see Maslow as compatible with the scriptural view of the self and supporting from a psychological framework the approach to spirituality I have been presenting. My faith view of the self easily sees the power of the Spirit in the entire process. His insistence on the essential goodness of our nature reflects my belief that God created us in God's own image, looked at us and all his creation, and saw that we were good. His insistence that we have a guide within our deepest nature to continually direct our choices toward growth reflects my belief that the Holy Spirit has joined our spirit and is continually influencing and leading us. His insistence that our lack of growth and our destructive inclinations come from ignoring our inner guidance reflects my belief that we have the freedom to move against the influence of the Spirit. In addition, it also means that I am responding to superficial pressures on me and am not truly in tune with my deepest self. My deepest self, the self-in-God, is still fundamentally trustworthy, but under the pressure of destructive forces both within and outside myself, I have chosen to move with a more superficial level of my being. The grace of Christ is still present and still prompting me toward good, but I have freely chosen to move against it.

In no way do I intend to underestimate the power of evil in the world and in myself; to do this is to simultaneously undervalue the power of our redemption in Christ. I simply want to insist that grace is stronger than sin, and because of this we can rely on its help at all times, continuing to trust the inner self-in-God. Sin comes from not relying on this inner guidance and from responding to other influences. With Maslow's model of the person as psychological basis, I think of spirituality as a continual process of the transformation of our human spirit by the Spirit of Jesus. I see the Spirit operating to reinforce the inherent positive thrust of our being toward God, and I see the Spirit also operating to transform those evil inclinations that move us from God and others. I believe there is a gentle interior thrust within us, God's Spirit and our spirit working together, continually moving us toward love and service of God and others. The goal of spirituality is to move always with this thrust.

Distrusting the Self: Spirituality as Repression

Perhaps the most prevalent theory of personality that embodies a basically negative and distrustful view of human nature is the psychoanalytic theory of Freud. Most of us are not Freudians and would find it impossible to explain his theory of personality, yet I find that his theory explains well the implicit, unarticulated assumptions many of us have toward human nature. Freud's theory has great value for understanding human behavior; like all personality theories it explains some aspects of our nature better than other theories. I am not attempting to criticize Freud's great contributions and insights. I am looking at the theory from only one perspective—whether it presents the inner core of the person as a reliable guide to behavior and so fundamentally trustworthy. It does not; thus, I believe that it is fundamentally incompatible with Christian revelation. It does not adequately reflect the Christian theology of creation and redemption. I believe the theory leads to an implicit distrust of human nature. When adopted by Christians, whether explicitly or implicitly, it results in an understanding of spirituality that is aimed primarily at repression—or at best control—of the inner self. The following is an extremely simplified and inadequate presentation of a small part of Freud's theory. I present it solely to help those of us who are influenced by it to better recognize ourselves and then to reexamine our attitudes in light of the Gospel.

Freud does posit the existence of an inner nature common to all people; however, this nature is essentially destructive and cannot be trusted. The classical Freudian theory posits three basic personality mechanisms: the id, ego, and superego. The id is the primary process in the person; it is the source from which the energy comes for the entire personality, comparable to Maslow's inner nature. It can be summarized as the pleasure principle in the person, seeking always to gratify instinctual demands arising in it as soon as possible. But since it seeks to gratify instinctual demands with no regard for the harmful effects to oneself or others, it cannot be trusted. Two mechanisms—the ego and superego—exist to mediate the blind, selfish, and often destructive demands of the id. The two work together. The ego is the rational principle in the person; it dialogues with reality outside the person and presents alternative and non-destructive ways to fulfill the demands of the id, thus relieving its stored-up tensions. In doing this it draws upon the superego, the moral code of the individual internalized from codes presented by parents and society. The ego and superego work together to regulate the blind impulses of the id, especially the sexual and aggressive impulses, and to direct them in a way that is not harmful to the individual or to society. But the id remains the primary process in the person, the fundamental source of energy; the ego and superego are secondary and reactive processes.

I believe that the Freudian theory—at least as I have presented it here—is basically incompatible with Christian revelation. The theory states that our inner nature is basically a thrust toward selfish satisfaction of instinctual demands with no regard for the welfare of others. It insists that the primary energy of the entire personality flows from this thrust of the id. The secondary processes are needed to temper its destructiveness, namely, the ego and the superego redirecting the essentially selfish thrust of the id toward constructive fulfillment approved by society. I see this view of the self as opposed to my belief that God created us in God's own image, essentially good, and that, in addition, he sent the Spirit to reinforce and strengthen this positive dynamism of our nature. The primary energy of our deepest self is toward good. Evil in us is a secondary reaction, occurring when we move against our deepest nature and yield to pressures of selfishness from superficial levels of our being or from our external environment. In Freud's view growth does not come from trusting and responding to the inner self but rather from either repressing or sublimating this inner self and by responding to secondary processes of the ego and superego. I believe that this view has disastrous implications for spirituality. Since our inner selves cannot be trusted, spirituality becomes an effort to repress, or at best control, an essentially evil nature and to direct our lives according to some external standard of perfection that has been presented to us. In this view grace is not stronger than sin in us; Christ has not truly redeemed us. Since we cannot trust our inner selves for guides, we must measure our perfection by the external criteria of the written code. We cannot rely on the power of the Spirit of Christ in our hearts to transform all the inclinations of our inner selves and lead us gently toward love and service of God and others. In a sense we are like Paul before he had been freed from the law of sin in him and was still enslaved to the external law.

A Spirituality of Being

I have included this rather lengthy discussion of psychological models of the self because this dimension has been very helpful for me personally in adequately understanding the heart of Christian spirituality. During the past twenty-five years I have held three different views of human nature, and they have had great effect on my understanding of spirituality. I don't believe that I held these views in a vacuum. I believe they characterized many of the people with whom I lived and can even be said to reflect stages through which Christians in general were passing. The first view was essentially Freudian though not consciously so. I saw human nature as basically sinful, dominated by the effects of original sin, and so not able to be trusted. My effort was to overcome this nature and to live according to some supernature. I directed my life toward measuring up to sets of external guides of perfection presented to me by my religious order and the Church. I gradually passed from this view to a much more positive view of myself and human nature, probably around the time of the Second Vatican Council. Maslow's approach to the goodness of human nature summed up this attitude, though I was not familiar with Maslow at the time. I began to feel that we human beings had the power within our natures to make this world a better place. I definitely moved away from a mentality dominated by feelings of sin and evil in myself to one of confidence in the powers given human nature by the Creator. If we tried hard enough, we could make this world a better place for everyone. There was, however, little acknowledgement of the need for God's help in this effort. During both these periods, I believe I was more influenced by a self-outside-God approach to spirituality. In the first period I was too sinful and God wouldn't dwell in me; in the second period, I didn't need God since God had given me all the strength I needed in creating my human nature with so much positive potential. In both, the Western model of spirituality that sees good deeds as initiated by our own efforts and then rewarded by God was predominant.

I believe that I passed into the third stage—the one I'm in now—about ten years ago. I was writing my dissertation and had chosen to compare two approaches to religious experience, those of Thomas Merton and of Abraham Maslow. I recall beginning the dissertation feeling that Maslow, who articulated what I had implicitly held about human nature for several years, would emerge as being very similar to Merton, even though he was an agnostic. The more I worked on the dissertation, the more their differences emerged. I ended the dissertation with a conclusion exactly opposite to the one I started with. Since that time I have grown in the appreciation of the role of the Holy Spirit in all personal growth. My psychological approach has been infused by a theology of human nature acknowledging its basic goodness flowing from creation in God's image and recognizing the all-pervasive presence and power of the Spirit of Christ flowing from the redemption.

It is my conviction that Christian spirituality can be adequately understood only if we have an accurate understanding of the person taken from both theology and psychology. I have presented models of the self from theology and from psychology that have been helpful to me in understanding spirituality. I have also presented two models of the self commonly held that seem to me to distort an understanding of spirituality. The approach to spirituality I am taking is often called a "spirituality of being" because it seeks only to bring to fullness the being the Father has created and the Son has redeemed. It does not seek to impose any particular practices unrelated to becoming what we have been created to be. At the heart of the entire process of coming to this fullness is the Holy Spirit, our sanctifier. It is now necessary to look further into the New Testament to see what we can validly expect from this presence of the Spirit of Christ among us.

Reflection Questions

1. List several good deeds you have done today. Explain God's role in them according to the scriptural model of the self and according to the Western model of the self. Explain your role according to the two models.

2. Give examples of attitudes to spirituality in yourself and in others that reflect a self-outside-God understanding of spirituality.

3. How has an attitude of basic distrust of the self influenced your understanding and practice of Christian spirituality? Give concrete examples from past and present.

4. Describe how your understanding of Christian spirituality has changed throughout the years. Compare and contrast your present approach with the approach presented here.

II RECOGNIZING
THE HOLY SPIRIT

In all Christian traditions the Holy Spirit is clearly presented as sanctifier. Since Jesus' resurrection the task of bringing the world to the Father has been entrusted to the Spirit. Even the word we use, *spirit*uality, reflects the centrality of the Spirit in bringing both individuals and the world as a whole under the reign of the Father. The Second Vatican Council reaffirmed this age-old Christian tradition. It asserted, first, that the Holy Spirit was the Church's sanctifier.

> When the work which the Father had given the Son to do on earth was accomplished, the Holy Spirit was sent on the day of Pentecost in order that he might sanctify the Church, and thus all believers would have access to the Father through Christ in the one Spirit. He is the Spirit of life, a fountain springing up to life eternal. Through him the Father gives life to men who are dead from sin, till at last he revives in Christ even their mortal bodies.[1]

In addition, the Council asserted that the Holy Spirit was also santifier for the world beyond the Church.

> All this holds true not only for Christians, but for all men of good will in whose hearts grace works in an unseen way. For since Christ died for all men, and since the ultimate vocation of man is in fact one, and divine, we ought to believe that the Holy Spirit in a manner known only to God offers to every man the possibilities of being associated with the paschal mystery.[2]

In short, wherever people are working for good, both within and outside the Christian Church, the Holy Spirit is present. Using the New

Testament, I will give the three main activities of the Spirit: the Spirit as unifier, as enlightener, and as enabler. I present these as very general principles. Nowhere in the New Testament is there anything approaching a summary of the work of the Spirit, but using these three principles I believe we can adequately appreciate the New Testament conviction that the Spirit of Jesus is now present and infusing every aspect of life. It is the presence of the Spirit that is the culmination of the resurrection and the source of our "new creation" in Jesus.

The Problem of Recognizing the Spirit

If there is any Christian truth that has gone unappreciated, it is the presence of the Holy Spirit in our activities. The fact of the presence is clear; the problem is that we don't recognize it. There are many reasons for this. The main reason, I believe, is that we live in a secular society which explains all truth, including its understanding of human behavior, in secular terms. It seems to be a fact that most psychologists, those people who deal directly with understanding human behavior, such as Maslow and Freud, are non-believers. They present all principles for human behavior in naturalistic terms. This is indeed valid from a scientific perspective, but we Christians, in turn, ought to add our faith vision to our explanations of behavior. But we don't; we have been conditioned by our society not to think beyond the naturalistic theories of personal behavior presented to us. Often the presence of another factor in behavior, the Holy Spirit, which cannot be isolated and named in scientific terms, presents itself as a contradiction to our natural knowledge; thus we tend to deny or resist it. Human nature for a secular mentality is not the self-in-God.

Another reason we don't recognize the Holy Spirit in our daily activities is that much of our spirituality has been dominated by a self-outside-God model. God is in his heaven; we are in our world. We see ourselves as the sole initiator and power behind all good acts. If God has any role, it is in rewarding us for our good deeds after we have done them. I believe that this has been a dominant Western approach to spirituality. In addition to a secularistic mentality, even our theological model of spirituality has removed God from any real awareness of the presence of the Spirit in human behavior. This Western approach to spirituality is our current version of the old heresy of Pelagianism. In responding to the heresy of Pelagianism as far back as the fifth century, the Christian Church has insisted not only that all of our good actions are performed in response to the active power of the Spirit in us but also that the very first desires and movements toward these actions arise in us from the presence of this Spirit. Wherever in our life there is a desire and a movement toward goodness, we can recognize the presence of the Spirit. Our entire theology of redemption by the grace of Christ, so clear in the New Testament, hinges on this theological conclusion. If we alone, unaided by the presence of the Spirit, were responsible for initiating the good we do, our salvation would not be a free gift from God but rather something we earned by our good deeds. Christ would be unnecessary. I believe that the combination of secularism and an implicit Pelagianism have kept us from giving adequate recognition to the all-pervasive presence and power of the Holy Spirit in our daily lives.

A footnote to this Christian belief should be quickly added. God's Spirit joins our spirit; it does not replace it. The good acts we perform are truly our acts, not simply acts of the Holy Spirit in us. The deepest part of the self is the spiritual dimension. From this center flows all our freedom and love; at this level we remain free to choose to move or not to move with the Spirit. The Holy Spirit is indeed active in us at all times drawing us toward greater love and service of God and others, but the Spirit does not control our response. That flows from our freedom. The good acts we do are truly our own because we have freely chosen to do them. So much are they our own acts that Christian tradition has always taught that we will be rewarded or punished eternally according to how we use this freedom. It should be added that the devil does not force us to do evil acts; if we are held guilty by God for an evil act, it is only to the extent that we have freely chosen to do the act. This is easier to understand by comparing it with a friendship. We are generally drawn toward feeling and acting in love toward our friends, yet we know that at any given moment for any number of reasons we may both feel and act against this love. And so it is with the Lord. In examining the work of the Spirit in us according to the New Testament, it is well to recall that we refer to a gentle prompting rather than an overriding compulsion. And the prompting always waits upon our choosing to become our act, though many of us are habitually so accustomed to make choices according to the direction of the Spirit that we don't have to make a conscious choice each time. This too is very similar to human relationships.

Spirit as Unifier

In the New Testament and Christian tradition the primary effect of the indwelling of the Spirit is union and love. This love has as its object God, as well as other people. Christian theological tradition has most often seen the Holy Spirit in the Trinity as the bond of love between the Father and the Son. Elaborating on this, theologians point out that the Spirit works outside the Trinity the same way the Spirit works within the Trinity. The primary effect of the Spirit acting in people, they conclude, will be love, both for one another and for God. The most popular Christian prayer to the Spirit reflects this conclusion: "Come, Holy Spirit, fill the hearts of your faithful and enkindle in them the fire of your divine love."

Perhaps the classic passage on the Holy Spirit and human love in the New Testament is from John. The passage is cherished by Christians because it makes God present wherever there is love, and love is such a deep and fulfilling human emotion.

> My dear people, let us love one another, since love comes from God and everyone who loves is begotten by God and knows God. Anyone who fails to love can never have known God, because God is love. . . . No one has ever seen God; but as long as we love one another God will live in us and his love will be complete in us because he lets us share his Spirit (1 Jn. 4:7–8, 12–13).

The passage identifies God as the source of love; it immediately unites us with the life of God when we share in the love he has for his people. It is especially important because the love used here applies equally within the Christian Church and outside it; wherever there is love, there is God. Further on in the same passage, John emphasizes his point even further by asserting that those who say they love God but hate their brothers are liars. We can recall that the connection between the love of God and the love of neighbor was emphasized by

Jesus himself in his insistence that the second commandment, to love
one another, was like the first, to love God. The internal unity between the two loves is seen even more clearly by an appreciation of
the role of the Holy Spirit as the source of both.

Paul echoes John in asserting both that all love comes from
God: ". . . the love of God has been poured into our hearts by the
Holy Spirit which has been given us" (Rom. 5:5). As in John, the
Spirit is the source of all love, but where John emphasizes the bond
the Spirit creates among people, Paul emphasizes the new bond the
Spirit creates between believers and God, that of children to their Fa-
ther. Paul contrasts this relationship with the previous Jewish rela-
tionship, that of slaves to the harsh law-giving God of the Old
Testament.

> Everyone moved by the Spirit is a son of God. The spirit you re-
> ceived is not the spirit of slaves bringing fear into your lives again;
> it is the spirit of sons, and it makes us cry out, "Abba, Father!"
> The Spirit himself and our spirit bear united witness that we are
> children of God (Rom. 8:14–16).

Not only did the Spirit establish this new relationship with the Father, but it is only through the Spirit that we can now adequately express this relationship.

> The Spirit too comes to help us in our weakness. For when we
> cannot choose words in order to pray properly, the Spirit himself
> expresses our plea in a way that could never be put into words,
> and God who knows everything in our hearts knows perfectly
> well what he means, and that the pleas of the saints expressed by
> the Spirit are according to the mind of God (Rom. 8:26–27).

In addition to presenting the Spirit as the source of unity between believers and the Father, Paul frequently presents the Spirit as
the bond of unity among the Christians themselves. We are all familiar with the comparison Paul makes between the Christian community and the human body.

> Bear with one another charitably, in complete selflessness, gentle-
> ness and patience. Do all you can to preserve the unity of the

Spirit by the peace that binds you together. There is one body, one
Spirit, just as you were all called into one and the same hope when
you were called (Eph. 4:2–5).

And, finally, in Paul's famous passage on love, the Spirit is presented
as the source of all human love. Paul had pointed out that the Spirit
gave different people different gifts, but the greatest gift of all is love
and the ability to live in love with all people.

If I give away all that I possess, piece by piece, and if I even let
them take my body to burn it, but am without love, it will do me
no good whatever. Love is always patient and kind; it is never
jealous; love is never boastful or conceited; it is never rude or selfish; it does not take offense, and is not resentful. Love takes no
pleasure in other people's sins but delights in the truth; it is always ready to excuse, to trust, to hope, and to endure whatever
comes (1 Cor. 13:3–7).

Paul clearly presents the Holy Spirit as the source of love and unity
between the believers and the Father, among the believers themselves, and finally as the source of love among all people, within or
outside the Christian community.

The New Testament message on love and the presence of the
Spirit is simple: where there is love there is God. The main problem
for me is not understanding the message but drawing out its implications for my life. Do I adequately acknowledge that the Spirit is present and working in me every time I move toward God or others in
love? Do I recognize the Spirit or do I attribute these movements
solely to my initiative? I can recognize the Spirit in my teaching,
counseling, writing, study, or helping others whenever I do these activities predominantly to love and serve the Lord. I can acknowledge
the Spirit's absence when I do these activities for purely selfish reasons or do them begrudgingly simply because they are expected of
me. I can also acknowledge the presence of the Spirit in my daily
prayer. If I have been moved toward the Lord during morning meditation or during the day or during Mass, I can recognize the Spirit
working within me to draw me toward God: his Spirit joins my spirit

and is continually moving me not only toward others but also toward God. I know that I am personally unaware of the extent of this movement in me. Almost every day some new aspect of the Spirit's work becomes clearer; what I had previously seen as only a natural phenomenon, I can now see as the work of the Spirit because love was present. I am also becoming more acutely aware when it is absent in me by lack of love, joy, and peace.

I am also beginning to realize that these conscious acknowledgements of the presence of the Spirit in my daily life are probably just the tip of the iceberg. Before these activities come to the point of being consciously acknowledged by me, the Spirit has been present deep in my heart, moving me on a level below conscious knowledge and reflection. Much as a husband is motivated by love for his wife and family during his work without specifically adverting to this fact, so am I in a deep and often unconscious way moved by the Spirit to perform more and more of my daily service in love.

And there is a very healthy side-effect to my personal recognition of the Spirit in my life: I begin to recognize the Spirit more and more in those around me. I can see the Spirit in students helping one another prepare for tests, supporting one another during lonely times away from home, making new friendships in the dorms, fraternities and sororities, donating blood to the Red Cross, or worshiping around the altar. I can recognize the Spirit in fellow faculty members spending long office hours to help students, working patiently on university committees to improve effectiveness of the structures, or just taking on another job in the department that needs to be done to make the place better for all. Perhaps the Spirit is least recognized and most present in national and international political figures laboring for justice and peace. I get a sense of greatness and love emanating from some of them making prodigious efforts for the sake of the world, often at the risk of their own health and life, that would be possible only with strength from the Holy Spirit. As I become more sensitive to the presence of the Spirit in those around me, I also seem to become more sensitive to the Spirit's absence in some. I find myself praying for the Spirit to come to those people and places; the daily newspaper and evening news are good places to recognize both the presence and absence of the Spirit in our world.

Spirit as Enlightener

Perhaps no aspect of the Spirit's work is more stressed in popular Christian tradition than the Spirit's role of enlightener and guider. This dimension is closely related to the role as unifier. The Spirit having united us with the Lord and others in love now guides us in the way to best express this love. The importance of this intellectual dimension of the Spirit's work is reflected in the traditional seven gifts of the Spirit; four of them are predominantly cognitive. These are gifts of wisdom, understanding, counsel, and knowledge. And this tradition is firmly rooted in the Gospel. Jesus called the Spirit he promised the disciples at the Last Supper the Spirit of truth.

> I shall ask the Father, and he will give you another Advocate to be with you for ever, that Spirit of truth whom the world can never receive since it neither sees nor knows him; but you know him because he is with you, he is in you (Jn. 14:16–17).

And then Jesus proceeded to explain what the disciples could expect from the presence of this Spirit within them.

> I have said these things to you while still with you; but the Advocate, the Holy Spirit, whom the Father will send in my name, will teach you everything and remind you of all I have said to you (Jn. 14:25–26).

Two aspects of this intellectual dimension of the Spirit's role stand out: enlightenment and guidance.

Paul presents the Spirit as enlightener in two ways. First, the Spirit enlightens believers, enabling them to recognize God as Father and Jesus as Lord. As we have seen, only after we have received the Spirit can we cry, "Abba, Father." Likewise, it is only through the Spirit that we can recognize Jesus himself as Lord.

> "I want you to understand that on the one hand no one can be speaking under the influence of the Holy Spirit and say, 'Curse Jesus,' and on the other hand, no one can say, 'Jesus is Lord' unless he is under the influence of the Holy Spirit" (1 Cor. 12:3).

Second, the Spirit enlightens us by giving us the ability to accept and understand all aspects of the teaching connected with this gift of faith in the Father and Jesus. Paul asserts that his ability to preach and his hearers' ability to understand both flow from the presence of the Spirit.

> Far from relying on any power of my own, I came among you in great "fear and trembling," and in my speeches and the sermons that I gave, there were none of the arguments that belong to philosophy, only a demonstration of the power of the Spirit. And I did this so that your faith should not depend on human philosophy but on the power of God.

> These are the very things that God has revealed to us through the Spirit, for the Spirit reaches the depths of everything, even the depths of God. After all, the depths of a man can only be known by his own spirit, not by any other man, and in the same way the depths of God can only be known by the Spirit of God. Now instead of the spirit of the world, we have received the Spirit that comes from God, to teach us to understand the gifts he has given us. Therefore we teach not in the way in which philosophy is taught, but in the way that the Spirit teaches us; we teach spiritual things spiritually. An unspiritual person is one who does not accept anything of the Spirit of God: he sees it all as nonsense; it is beyond his understanding because it can only be understood by means of the Spirit (1 Cor. 2:4–14).

The other intellectual aspect of the Spirit's role is guidance. Here also two activities are given. First, the Spirit is presented in Paul as giving guidance to direct the consciences of believers.

> Let me put it like this: if you are guided by the Spirit you will be in no danger of yielding to self-indulgence, since self-indulgence is the opposite of the Spirit, the Spirit is totally against such a thing, and it is precisely because the two are so opposed that you do not carry out your good intentions (Gal. 5:16–17).

Paul then contrasts the effects of self-indulgence with the effects of the Spirit.

> When self-indulgence is at work the results are obvious: fornica-
> tion, gross indecency and sexual irresponsibility; idolatry and sor-
> cery; feuds and wrangling, jealousy, bad temper and quarrels;
> disagreements, factions, envy; drunkenness, orgies and similar
> things. . . . What the Spirit brings is very different: love, joy,
> peace, patience, kindness, goodness, trustfulness, gentleness, and
> self-control. . . . You cannot belong to Christ Jesus unless you
> crucify all self-indulgent passions and desires (Gal. 5:19–20, 22,
> 24).

He concludes the discussion simply: "Since the Spirit is our life, let
us be directed by the Spirit" (Gal. 5:25). For Paul allowing the Spirit
to direct his conscience toward good was a new principle of morality.
Before the reception of the Spirit, he had been guided solely by the
external law. He exhorts his listeners to serve God now in a new
way, to follow the law written on their hearts and not merely the
written law: "But now we are rid of the law, freed by death from our
imprisonment, free to serve in the new spiritual way and not the old
way of a written law" (Rom. 7:6). We should recall that Paul does
not claim that the Spirit will take away the tendencies toward self-
indulgence within us. He claims only that we need not be dominated
by them because of the presence of the new power of the Spirit.
Christ has redeemed us from the power of sin. And Paul knew from
experience the difference between being under the law and under the
Spirit. The law had no power to free from selfishness and sin; only
the Spirit could do that.

And there is a second way that the Spirit is presented in the
New Testament as giving guidance. The Spirit is occasionally shown
as illuminating individuals to make practical choices according to
God's will between two courses of action. This facet of guidance is
not as developed as the first. Later Christian tradition, however, has
elaborated these foundations into a theology of discernment. One example of this role of the Spirit in helping discover God's will is the
very important decision made by the early community not to be
bound by Jewish dietary laws and, by implication, all other Jewish
laws. The apostles and elders of Jerusalem support their decision
with the authority of the Holy Spirit in announcing it to the non-
Jewish Christians.

> It has been decided by the Holy Spirit and by ourselves not to sad-
> dle you with any burden beyond these essentials: you are to ab-
> stain from food sacrificed to idols, from blood, from the meat of
> strangled animals and from fornication (Acts 15:28–29).

There are indications in the New Testament that the early community was in the habit of praying to the Spirit for guidance in important
decisions, and of seeing decisions as arising from the Spirit's guidance within them. One such example is Paul's decision to go to Jerusalem to reconcile differences with the Jerusalem church.

> But now as you see, I am on my way to Jerusalem, compelled by
> the Spirit and not knowing what will happen to me there—except
> that the Holy Spirit has been warning me from city to city that
> chains and hardships await me there (Acts 20:22–23, in *New
> American Bible*).

It is interesting to note that the Spirit seems to have prompted Paul's
friends in an opposite way regarding the trip: "Under the Spirit's
promptings they tried to tell Paul that he should not go up to Jerusalem, but to no purpose" (Acts 21:4, in *New American Bible*). But
even in their disagreement, the two passages testify that the community was used to looking to the Spirit for guidance in making practical decisions according to God's will.

We have discussed two effects of the Holy Spirit in us. The first
effect, the Spirit as unifier, stresses the affective dimensions of the
Spirit, the Spirit's role in uniting us in love with God and other people. The second effect, the Spirit as enlightener, stresses the cognitive
dimensions of the Spirit's work. In fact, the two effects will be present together. We know that human beings operate as a unity; one dimension cannot be separated from the other: we know and love
simultaneously. The Spirit in us likewise transforms all the dimensions of our being simultaneously; for instance, we must know the
Lord through the gift of faith before we can love and serve him in all
our actions. I have separated the different effects of the Spirit in us
only in order to discuss them systematically. As I discuss recognizing
the Spirit as enlightener in daily life, it will become clear that the

Spirit guides us always toward greater union and love with God and others.

It is clear that the Spirit's activity as enlightener covers a vast range of areas in our life. Because this activity is so all-pervasive, it becomes hard to recognize concretely in daily situations. I believe that I am most aware of these effects in the following four areas of my life. Perhaps the most dominant effect is the Spirit's role in guiding my conscience. I make formal examinations of conscience twice a day, at noon and at night. During these times I review all my activities to see if I have been following the Spirit's promptings or merely my own. By checking my dispositions against the criteria given in Paul, I can recognize where the Spirit has been present. If I have been dominated by love, peace, patience, and kindness, I know the Spirit was present; if I have been dominated by anxiety, quarrels, jealousy, and hatred, I know I have not been under the influence of the Spirit. Second, I am beginning to recognize the presence of the Spirit in helping me understand better the truths of revelation. I am a theologian, so this is an important area of my life. There are many different theories on Christ, redemption, and original sin, and it is hard to know which ones to teach at length. In choosing the position I will espouse and teach, I always pray to the Spirit for enlightenment. I find myself subtly being moved toward one approach. I used to think this occurred only because of my studious theological investigations; now I believe that my understanding is also influenced by the Spirit. Third, I spend a good deal of time doing personal and spiritual counseling. While attentively listening to the other person, I often find myself intuiting the person's situation and prompted to ask the question that is just right for helping the person grasp the situation better. In responding to questions in class and talks I give, I also believe that frequently I am led by the Spirit to respond appropriately.

Finally, I can recognize the Spirit's guidance in discerning God's will in my service, though not connected with right or wrong moral decisions. I believe that if the decision has to do with greater love and service of God and others, the Spirit will guide me. I experience this guidance in deciding small things, such as which courses to teach and speaking engagements to accept, as well as in making larger decisions, such as whether to stay or move from my present apostolate, to apply for a sabbatical, or to write this book. In making these decisions, I generally use one of the Ignatian methods for discerning God's will. Having decided that a particular decision is God's will, I am better able to throw myself into it wholeheartedly.

The experiences I have presented are from my own life. Since I am a priest and theologian, it may appear that the Spirit works only within these narrow limits. This is surely not the implication of the New Testament. The Spirit is working in every believer, in every area of life. Wherever we are conscientiously striving to love and serve God and others, the Spirit is present. And the Spirit is also present outside the Christian community in all human beings, whenever they are motivated by love. I believe that we Christians have the challenge of holding our daily activities against the message of the New Testament and asking God to help us understand how his Spirit has been at work all the time, though perhaps unrecognized by us. Likewise, we have the challenge of acknowledging those aspects of our life that are not under the dominance of the Spirit. As I have become more sensitive to the Spirit's work in me, I am recognizing more and more the Spirit's work in others. It is a great support to my faith and a great motive for praising God in prayer to recognize his Spirit in students, faculty, friends, and national and international figures. This recognition, since it leads to greater love of God, is also the work of the Spirit.

Spirit as Enabler

Another role assigned by Christian tradition to the Spirit is not adequately represented in the above discussion: the role of the Spirit as enabler, as the source of strength to serve God and others. This role complements the first two. The Spirit first unifies us with the Lord and other people, then guides us in how best to serve, and finally completes the work by giving us the strength to serve. This tradition is best embodied in our understanding of the sacrament of confirmation. Confirmation is the sacrament which gives strength for Christians to assume their adult roles in the community; after confirmation we are expected to assume responsibility for the faith in a new way by becoming active witnesses to the Gospel or, in popular terminology, "soldiers of Christ." This tradition is represented among the seven gifts of the Holy Spirit in the gift of fortitude.

These activities of the Spirit as enabler seem most clear in the New Testament. First, the Spirit is presented as giving the first Christians strength to witness to the Gospel even at the cost of their lives. This effect is present in the New Testament more by implication than by direct discussion. The Pentecost event, and indeed the entire account of the Acts of the Apostles, show the new power that the disciples received after the reception of the Spirit. We recall that the death of Jesus had stunned the disciples. They were gathered one night behind locked doors for fear that what happened to Jesus might also happen to them. Then came the sound of wind and tongues of fire, and they were "filled with the Holy Spirit and began to speak foreign languages as the Spirit gave them the gift of speech" (Acts 2:4, in *New American Bible*). Incident after incident in the Acts of the Apostles reflects the new strength they received to preach and witness to the Gospel even amid persecution. The Spirit is presented not only as giving strength but also as giving the content of the message to be preached: "Then Peter, filled with the Holy Spirit, addressed them. . . ." (Acts 4:8, in *New American Bible*). Before his death Jesus had assured them that they would receive this special help in times of trial.

> "But when they hand you over, do not worry about how to speak or what to say; what you are to say will be given to you when the time comes; because it is not you who will be speaking; the Spirit of your Father will be speaking in you" (Mt. 10:19–20).

Second, the Spirit is presented as giving Christians the power to perform their special roles within the Christian community for the building up of the community. These gifts, or charisms, transform the natural capacities of the person and enable them to be used more effectively for the good of the whole group. Every person, as a member of the body of Christ, is seen as having some particular function to perform for the good of the whole body. The Holy Spirit is present enabling the individual to perform the function well.

> There is a variety of gifts but always the same Spirit; there are all sorts of service to be done, but always to the same Lord; working in all sorts of different ways in different people, it is the same God

who is working in all of them. The particular way in which the Spirit is given to each person is for a good purpose. One may have the gift of preaching with wisdom given him by the Spirit; another may have the gift of preaching instruction given him by the same Spirit; and another the gift of faith given by the same Spirit; another the gift of healing, through this one Spirit; one, the power of miracles; another, prophecy; another the gift of recognizing spirits; another the gift of tongues and another the ability to interpret them. All these are the work of one and the same Spirit, who distributes different gifts to different people just as he chooses (1 Cor. 12:4–11).

Finally, the Spirit is presented as having a special role in strengthening believers to work for the poor outside the Christian community. This is seen most dramatically in the Gospels. The Messiah promised that the Jews would be filled with the Spirit of God and, as a result, work tirelessly for all, especially the disadvantaged. Jesus identified himself with this mission of the Messiah.

> The spirit of the Lord has been given to me, for he has anointed me. He has sent me to bring the good news to the poor, to proclaim liberty to captives and to the blind new sight, to set the downtrodden free, to proclaim the Lord's year of favor (Lk. 4:18–19).

This same Spirit that made Jesus so zealous for the poor is now present in the Christian community, guiding and enabling us also to work for the poor and oppressed.

I believe that I can recognize the Spirit in me, enabling me to work zealously both within the Christian community and in the world. First in the community, I recognize the Spirit's role in strengthening me in my work as a teacher. I see the Spirit as enabling me to perform this particular task for the sake of building up the Christian community. Often when I am tired or discouraged, I seem to receive new strength by relying on my belief that I have been given this task for the sake of the community and can count on the special help and presence of the Spirit to do it well. I believe that the Spirit also infuses my work as a priest, especially my preaching at Mass. There are times when I am able to express myself in a homily far beyond anything I had prepared. Second, in my work outside the community, I have come to recognize the Spirit in my life by a new restlessness and concern to work for the underprivileged and for peace and justice. I have become involved in several social actions in response to this movement. As I become more aware of how the Spirit is working in me to help me fulfill my roles in the Christian community and the world, I become more aware of the Spirit working in others to help them fulfill their roles. I am ever impressed by the endless patience and kindness of a mother with young children as well as with the patience and persistence of some national and world leaders. I am moved by the long hours that university administrators put in to improve some small aspect of university functioning as well as by the patience and kindness of my faculty colleagues in remaining in their offices and explaining a point for the hundredth time to whoever comes. All these activities when performed in love demand the special presence and strength of the Spirit. In all these activities, the Spirit is working simultaneously unifying, enlightening, and enabling us to serve God and others.

The Holy Spirit: The Spirit of Jesus

It can be rightly objected that dividing the Spirit's activity in us into three different spheres is really a distortion of the Spirit's work. The activity can be presented much more simply: the Spirit works in us as the Spirit worked in Christ. We know that the Gospels present Jesus as being completely under the influence of the Spirit. Jesus was conceived by the Spirit, was baptized with the Spirit, and lived his life under the influence of the Spirit. We know that at the Last Supper Jesus promised to send his Spirit to his disciples, assuring them that it was better for them that he himself left, for this was necessary for the Spirit to come. We know that this promise was fulfilled when the Spirit of Jesus descended upon the disciples at Pentecost. Having received Jesus' Spirit, the disciples become for the first time children of the Father, sharing now in Jesus' relationship with the Father. Christian spirituality now formally begins; the Spirit of Jesus now works in the believers to make them ever more like Jesus. This gives us our ultimate criterion for recognizing the Spirit in ourselves and in others: we recognize the Spirit working in us to the extent that we are like Christ.

In discussing the role of the Spirit in helping us become like Christ, it is important to clarify what this does not mean. It does not mean having the inclinations and temptations to sin taken away from us. Christ himself was tempted. We become like Christ in temptations by responding to them as he did; we have the power to overcome them because he has given us his Spirit. Nor does becoming like Christ mean denying our unique personality characteristics to adopt some external facade that appears holy to others. It means allowing our unique personal traits to be influenced by the Spirit—as were Christ's—and so be directed always toward love and service. Nor, finally, does becoming like Christ mean being removed from our particular vocation in life to live in some removed, sacred environment in which we can praise God undisturbed. Rather it means performing all the duties of our vocation under the influence of the Spirit. In short, we can become like Christ and still remain who we are, where we are.

Living under the influence of the Spirit of Christ and becoming like Christ surely does mean one thing: being forever concerned and active in the world to promote the Father's kingdom. Reading the Gospels one gets the impression of Christ as a person continually on the move, putting in a full day's work and retiring at night exhausted. The impression of the first Christian community is also one of continual activity for the sake of the Gospel. The Spirit's presence in Christ and in the community impelled them ever outward. Too often the Spirit's presence has been identified with a type of peaceful resting in the Lord, removed from the distractions of daily life. This is surely not the image given by the New Testament. Jesus and the first community experienced peace, joy, and love, but this peace and joy is presented as accompanying their activity for the Father, rather than as found in personal isolation. In our day when we Christians are becoming more and more conscious of our responsibility for transforming the unjust structures of our society through active involvement in society, this is an important criterion to keep in mind.

The most encouraging aspect of the New Testament message on the Spirit is that the Spirit has been working in our lives all along; we

III THE HOLY SPIRIT AND PERSONAL PRAYER

The Holy Spirit is our sanctifier. This means that the Spirit is active in all our approaches toward God, whether they be in our daily service or in our prayer. Just as we do not adequately recognize the role of the Spirit in daily life, so also we do not fully appreciate the importance of the Spirit's role in prayer; our secular and Pelagian mentality dominates our understanding of prayer. I believe that a renewed understanding of prayer comes only when we acknowledge the Spirit's role and then learn to respect it in practice. By *prayer* let us understand any expression of our relationship to God done under the influence of the Holy Spirit. This expression occurs in two ways. The first and primary way we express our relationship with God is by our spontaneous prayers throughout the day during our actions. As we begin to recognize God in ourselves and in others, we begin to see all our activities in reference to him. Then we spontaneously begin dialogue with him during these activities, such as thanking him for his help or asking him for strength. Jesus gives a good example of this type of personal prayer in the Gospels. The disciples had just returned from a successful missionary journey and were enthusiastically telling Jesus about it. Luke records the spontaneous prayer that burst from Jesus' heart—under the influence of the Spirit.

> It was then that, filled with joy by the Holy Spirit, he said, "I bless you, Father, Lord of heaven and of earth, for hiding these things from the learned and the clever and revealing them to mere children. Yes, Father, for that is what it pleased you to do" (Lk. 10:21).

The second general way we express this relationship is by formally withdrawing from our daily activities to be with the Lord, whether in personal prayer, shared prayer, or liturgical prayer. All three forms of withdrawal are important for a balanced life of formal prayer. We will focus our attention primarily on personal prayer, since this is the area that is most often misunderstood. The principles discussed apply to shared prayer and liturgical prayer also, but I will be using them mainly to refer to personal prayer—what Jesus did so often in the Gospels when he left the crowds and went by himself to the mountain or the desert. My understanding of personal prayer has been helped most by Thomas Merton. I will present five themes which I believe reflect his own final thought and which also synthesize my own insights. These themes are the following: prayer as letting the Spirit speak, as an expression of the whole self, as an experience of the whole self, as discovering God in oneself, and as resting in the Lord. The purpose of this chapter is to present an understanding of prayer that flows from the scriptural model of the self. The practical implications for praying will be discussed in the following chapter.

Prayer as Letting the Spirit Speak

Personal prayer is our expression of our relationship with God under the influence of the Holy Spirit. I believe it is the latter half of the description that is most misunderstood. Scripture is clear in insisting that we cannot be united with God without the help of his Spirit. Strings of words and thoughts we compose that are not brought under this influence have not really entered into the realm of true prayer. Many people express this problem by saying that in their personal prayer they seem to be "talking to themselves." This understanding of prayer, highlighting the centrality of the role of the Spirit, is presented most clearly by Paul in the Epistle to the Romans; nowhere else does the New Testament present so succinctly the inner dynamic of our union with the Lord in prayer. Paul had just pointed out that Christians, through the reception of the Spirit, existed in an entirely new relationship with God; they were God's adopted children. This intimacy was not true for the Jews—nor for any other religion in the world. How, then, could this new relationship be adequately expressed? Not by their own unaided efforts, Paul insists.

> The Spirit too comes to help us in our weakness. For when we cannot choose words in order to pray properly, the Spirit himself expresses our plea in a way that could never be put into words, and God who knows everything in our hearts knows perfectly well what he means, and that the pleas of the saints expressed by the Spirit are according to the mind of God (Rom. 8:26–27).

Jesus did not give much formal teaching on prayer, but one of the few points he did make was that our prayers should not be characterized by many words, as were those of the pagans and Pharisees.

> In your prayers do not babble as the pagans do, for they think that by using many words they will make themselves heard. Do not be like them; your Father knows what you need before you ask him (Mt. 6:2–8).

The implication is that many words are not needed because the Holy Spirit will make known to our Father all we need. After these remarks, Jesus taught the disciples the Our Father. It should be noted that in the New Testament both the prayer of Jesus and the prayers of the first Christians were directed primarily to God the Father. Since the Spirit is the bond of union between the Father and the Son, it is clear that the Spirit will direct the hearts of Christians with the Son to the Father. But the Spirit is also the bond of all our union in prayer. In the epistles we find Christians praying to Jesus as well as to the Father; the Spirit is, after all, the Spirit of Jesus and can be expected to draw Christians to the Lord. The Spirit of Jesus can also be expected to draw us to Jesus' mother, Mary; and so very soon Christians begin praying to Mary. Finally, the Spirit is the bond of union among all Christians, living and dead. The Spirit, then, can unite us in love with all the great saints of God and direct us in prayer to them to make intercession for us with the Father. It should be noted, however, that Christians praying under the influence of the Spirit will find their prayers directed primarily toward the Father and Jesus; they will find that prayers to Mary and the saints will be for the sake of greater union with Jesus and the Father.

My personal understanding of prayer has not always respected the centrality of the Spirit. I believe that I, and many Christians I knew, were led to a misunderstanding of prayer by not adequately grasping two common definitions of prayer we were taught. We understood them both as being accomplished without the Holy Spirit, in a self-outside-God model of the person. I was taught that prayer was "conversation with Christ." I erroneously understood this to mean that as in ordinary human conversation my role was to compose the script, and if the script was well composed and contained appropriate words, thoughts, images, feelings, and resolutions, Christ would reward me with an experience of his presence. But the outcome of the prayer was essentially in my hands. I was also taught that prayer was "raising my heart and mind to God." Again I erroneously understood this to mean that it was solely by my own effort that my heart would be raised, and that if I did this well God would make God's presence known. In both misunderstandings, I saw myself as initiating all movement to God; God's role was to reward me with personal consolation. In both I saw prayer as primarily verbal and depending on correct use of my intellectual powers; I was anxious if there was too much silence and would eagerly begin a new string of thoughts to achieve my goal of consolation. I had misunderstood these two common definitions, for both can be understood correctly from a self-in-God model, as long as we acknowledge that if we truly enter into union and dialogue with Jesus and the Father, the Spirit has been present and working in us. In a correct understanding of these traditional descriptions of prayer, we see ourselves as establishing the right conditions through proper use of our body and minds so that we can be attentive to the Spirit and allow the Spirit of Jesus to draw us into conversation with Jesus and to raise our hearts and minds toward our Father.

I believe I learned the lesson that prayer depended primarily on the movement of the Spirit in me and not on my own intellectual efforts the first time I tried to use the Jesus Prayer. The Jesus Prayer consists of repeating rather slowly, and sometimes coordinated with breathing, the following phrase: "Lord Jesus Christ, Son of God, have mercy on me, a sinner." I had heard about this traditional prayer but had always been afraid to try it. In addition, I had heard about mantra prayers similar to it, short phrases from Scripture repeated slowly and sometimes coordinated with breathing. I had also heard of praying by repeating only one word, such as "Jesus," "Father," or "Love." One day I tried it for my morning meditation. Breathing in I prayed, "Lord Jesus Christ," breathing out I prayed, "Son of God," breathing in, "have mercy on me," breathing out, "a sinner." Nothing happened. First I was too distracted by the new method. Second, in my heart I did not feel it would work; I felt I should be doing more—more thoughts, more acts of love. I tried it a second day. I found I was very peaceful and not questioning the method as much. I thought there might even be a real presence of God, but I wasn't sure. It seemed that this presence could just be coincidental. I tried it the third day. Within a few minutes I was peacefully in the presence of God, slowly and rhythmically repeating the words of the prayer. I began using the prayer daily, and the presence of God continued to accompany it. Then I changed the prayer and used one of my favorite Scripture phrases the same way: "I am the vine, you are the branches; without me, you can do nothing." A gentle presence of the Lord again emerged. These experiences revolutionized my understanding of prayer. For the first time, I acknowledged that the result of prayer was in the Lord's hands. In repeating these simple phrases, there was no clever use of thoughts or images; I had to conclude that the primary reason for the success of my prayer was the work of the Spirit in me. I also concluded that the primary reason for the success of the prayers in the past was also the Spirit, and not my own intelligent use of personal insights on praying well. Understanding prayer now through the self-in-God model, I realize that my role is to provide the conditions which enable me to be sensitive to the Spirit within me. I simply respond to this movement. If in prayer I am gifted with a new sense of God's presence, I now thank the Lord, rather than congratulate myself.

Thomas Merton is a great help in understanding this approach to personal prayer. He continually repeats that prayer is essentially the work of the Spirit in us. We must get out of the way so that God can produce the effect he desires.

It can therefore be said that the aim of mental prayer is to awaken the Holy Spirit within us, and to bring our hearts into harmony with his voice, so that we allow the Holy Spirit to speak and pray within us, and lend him our voice and our affections that we may become, as far as possible, conscious of his prayer in our hearts.[1]

Merton always acknowledges that our efforts remain necessary, but they ought to be directed toward putting us in tune with the Holy Spirit. As we grow in prayer, our own efforts diminish before the action of the Spirit. But even for the beginner, the attempt must be to allow the Spirit to move as It wills.

> The activity of the Spirit within us becomes more and more important as we progress in the life of interior prayer. It is true that our own efforts remain necessary, at least as long as they are not entirely superseded by the action of God "in us and without us" (according to a traditional expression). But more and more our efforts attain a new orientation: instead of being directed toward ends we have chosen ourselves, instead of being measured by the profit and pleasure we judge they will produce, they are more and more directed to an obedient and cooperative submission to grace, which implies first of all an increasingly attentive and receptive attitude toward the hidden activity of the Holy Spirit.[2]

Merton continually stresses that the result of prayer is always a gift. This separates Christian prayer from psychological techniques that produce effects commensurate with personal efforts at concentration, such as transcendental meditation.

> And so the contemplation of which I speak is a religious and transcendent gift. It is not something to which we can attain alone, by intellectual effort, by perfecting our natural powers. It is not a kind of self-hypnosis resulting from concentration on our own inner spiritual being. It is not the fruit of our own efforts.[3]

And we have every reason to expect that God will give us this gift of prayer and even the advanced prayer of contemplation. We must trust our deepest selves, the self united with the Spirit, and await expectantly both in prayer and outside prayer for this gift.

> It [the contemplative life] is always something for which we must learn how to wait but it is also something which we must learn to

expect actively. The secret of the contemplative life is in this *ability for active awareness,* an active and expectant awareness where the activity is a deep personal response on a level which is, so to speak, beyond the faculties of the soul.[4]

It is important to note that these times of increased awareness of God's presence with us will occur both during formal prayer and also spontaneously during our daily life. A person who is continually attentive to the movement of the Spirit may find that they occur more frequently outside formal prayer times, much like Luke's report of Jesus' experience of breaking into praise of the Father at the disciples' return from this first missionary journey.

Prayer as an Expression of the Whole Self

We have been describing prayer as our expression of our relationship to God under the influence of the Holy Spirit. It is important to emphasize that prayer must be an authentic expression, flowing from the center of our being and of our life. In fact, prayer could be called the most fundamental expression of our identity, for both by creation and by grace we human beings exist to be fulfilled completely only through our relationship with the Lord. Prayer to our God is the human act par excellence, as natural and spontaneous to our being as love of one another. Unfortunately, this truth has not always been respected.

First, there has been a tendency in the past to see prayer as the expression of but one part of our being. We had the tendency to see nature and grace as independent sources of activity and unconnected with each other. Since prayer had God as its object, it had to flow from the supernatural dimension of our being, a dimension not necessarily connected with our natural activities. Our natural activities had their own natural objects, unconnected with the supernatural realm of the soul. We know now that we human beings operate as a unity in all we do. When the Holy Spirit comes to us, it comes at the deepest level of our being, the level of spirit: God's Spirit joins our spirit. From this center the Spirit moves out, transforming the other two levels of our being, the mind and the body. All our human activities, physical, psychological and spiritual, can fall under the influence of the Spirit. The accompanying model is helpful:

The Human Being

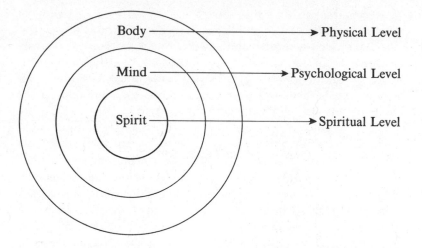

Our prayer to God, then, is a deep, authentic human movement done under the prompting of the Spirit, flowing from our deepest personal center and affecting our physical and mental activities. Once we grasp this, prayer becomes easier; we become convinced that we can move to the Lord in a natural and spontaneous way. Prayer need not be something difficult or at odds with the deepest dimension of our being, accomplished only by striving mightily to overcome and control a basically sinful self.

Second, if personal prayer is to be an authentic expression of our relationship with God, it must flow from the center of our daily life. There has been a tendency in the past to see formal prayer as concerned with a very narrow realm of human life, even to remove it from daily life and situate it within a supposed sacred realm. We would find ourselves praying for virtues which were supposedly necessary in the supernatural life but which had no appeal for us. We would force ourselves to become concerned with aspects of the Gospel that were judged necessary for a balanced Christian life. These aspects might be neatly arranged in a meditation book and presented to us systematically over a period of a year. Each day we tried to allow the Holy Spirit to move us to God from this starting point. Often it did not work. We would make prodigious efforts to get interested in the meditation topics, but nothing would happen. In effect, we would not be asking the Holy Spirit to join our spirit and raise us to God. We were putting our spirit aside and praying as if it were unimportant. Our daily concerns were bracketed; we tried to reach God apart from where we truly were. I believe the result was that prayer became frustrating and boring, a duty we had to perform to be holy, a duty for which we earned much grace precisely because it was so difficult. It was not a natural and authentic expression of our deepest self under the influence of the Spirit.

I recall quite clearly when my attitude toward personal prayer changed from being a rather burdensome daily duty to a spontaneous expression of my relationship to the Lord. I was working as a teacher at an Indian mission in South Dakota. Each day we arose at 5:00 A.M. and spent forty-five minutes in personal prayer. The time was usually uneventful for me, due to tiredness, cold, and lack of interest in the topics I was praying over. My life at the mission was very difficult and often frustrating. I began taking walks down the highway at night alone to talk over my discouragement with the Lord. I looked forward to these walks and would not miss them if at all possible. After expressing my concerns, I recall growing quiet and experiencing a presence of the Lord. This presence made it all worthwhile, and I would leave the walk desiring to continue to serve him in this difficult situation. But for the greater part of the time at the mission I did not consider this personal prayer. I continued my rather fruitless morning meditations on my appropriate prayer topics. I soon needed sleep so badly that I decided to stay in bed during meditation time, rationalizing that I would not have the energy to serve God during the day if I didn't get more sleep and that I was at least spending time at night with him walking down the road. But my conscience did bother me for skipping something as important as daily meditation. One day during this period I had, at last, the realization that I was not skipping daily meditation; I was doing it at night. From that point on my attitude toward personal prayer changed. I now look forward to it and would find it impossible to live well without the regular daily experience of being with the Lord. Prayer, for the most part, has become easy and as spontaneous as expressing myself to a friend. I now allow God's Spirit to join mine and raise my heart easily and naturally to the Father and Jesus.

Merton well witnesses to the truth that prayer is an expression of our entire being and not simply one aspect of it. His approach to spirituality has been called a "spirituality of being" for the reason that he stresses the goal of becoming only what we have been created to be by the Lord, with the help of the Spirit.

> According to the scholastic maxim, *actio sequitur esse*, action is in accordance with the being that acts. As the Lord himself said, you cannot gather figs from thistles. Hence we must first be transformed interiorly into new men, and then act according to the Spirit given us by God, the Spirit of our new life, the Spirit of Christ.[5]

For Merton the application of this truth to personal prayer is clear. Prayer in the Christian transformed by the Spirit is the most fundamental expression of our identity as creature to our Creator. In his last written thoughts on prayer given in a sermon in Darjeeling, India, the month before he died, he summed up this truth.

> Prayer is an expression of who we are; our very being expresses itself with prayer because prayer flows from our relation to God and to other people and even . . . to all living things. Prayer comes from a deep sense of our incompleteness as creatures from the moment that we become aware that we are creatures and that our life is passing away and that we will all soon be dead. We realize that something has to give meaning to our life and that something cannot be merely our own. We are a living incompleteness. We are a gap, an emptiness that calls for fulfillment from someone else, and the very nature of our being as creatures implies this sense of a need to be completed by him from whom we come.[6]

Merton also insisted that prayer must be rooted in life and flow from life. Long before his final conversion Merton learned this truth. He had just graduated from high school and was traveling in Europe. His father had died the previous year; he himself had been seriously ill and had spent time in a sanatorium recovering from gangrene. He was currently leading a rather sinful life. In the solitude of a church in Rome he had a profound insight into his own existence. He prayed, he says, for the first time in his life.

> And now I think for the first time in my whole life I began to pray—praying not with my lips and my intellect and my imagination, but praying out of the very roots of my life and my being, and praying to the God I had never known, to reach down toward me out of his darkness and to help me to get free of the thousand terrible things that held my will in their slavery.[7]

In his final book on prayer Merton reflects on the importance of the spiritual life and personal prayer being part of everyday life.

> A false supernaturalism which imagines that "the supernatural" is a kind of Platonic realm of abstract essences totally apart from and opposed to the concrete world of nature offers no real support to a genuine life of meditation and prayer. Meditation has no point and no reality unless it is firmly rooted in *life*.[8]

Prayer as an Experience of the Whole Self

It would not be necessary to discuss this dimension of prayer if we had not subtly undervalued it in the past. Since prayer is a human activity, we can expect that it will have an experiential dimension, for we operate as a unity in all we do: our bodies, minds, and spirits working as one. Since prayer is primarily the expression of a relationship, we can expect that the experiential dimension will be even greater. Relationships are concrete personal categories that imply personal experiences, and the Lord presents himself to us in these categories, as Father, as Brother, as Friend and Helper. Since our relationship to the Lord is such a profound aspect of our being, we can expect that the experience of this relationship will also be profound. In the past, I believe we undervalued the experiential dimension for two reasons. First, we separated our supernatural activities from our natural ones and felt that the two activities operated in separate realms. Second, we overstressed the intellectual component of the faith, seeing it primarily as the acceptance of truths of revelation rather than the acceptance of the reality of Jesus as Lord and God as

Father. We now more correctly put the acceptance of the truths within the context of belief in the persons of the Father and Jesus. In learning to pray more effectively, it is essential that we learn to trust the deep inner experiences of our being because it is at this level that the Holy Spirit moves us. Taking these experiences seriously, we gradually learn to recognize where the Holy Spirit is working and distinguish that from where the Spirit is absent. This recognition is crucial for personal prayer.

How can we recognize the Spirit in personal prayer? Very simply, any movement of our heart toward God is from the Spirit. But we must acknowledge the fact that these movements will be experienced by us in a variety of different ways; the spiritual level at which the Spirit works will resonate differently on the levels of our minds and bodies. We must learn to recognize the Spirit within many different types of experiences. Two ways in which the Spirit moves are easy to recognize and accept. First, the Spirit's movements in us can be accompanied by feelings of happiness and sensible consolation. During prayer we are moved toward great gratitude to God for taking care of us and being our Father; this affects our feelings and gives us joy that we experience emotionally. Second, the Spirit's movement may be accompanied not so much by great sensible consolation as by a quiet inner peace in which we realize that God is present and loves us. We recognize the Spirit in the strong faith conviction. We can oversimplify and say that in the first experience the effects of the Spirit flow over clearly into our bodily dimension, and in the second experience they flow over primarily into our psychological dimension. These two types of experiences are easy to accept, and it is easy to recognize the Spirit in them because we are clearly being drawn closer to the Father. They are common in prayer.

But two other ways the Spirit works are more difficult to recognize and accept, and these are also common in prayer. We may experience the Lord as absent in our prayer; there is no feeling or conviction of his presence. We are aware only of our desire that he be present. In this deep desire coming from our heart, we can recognize the presence of the Spirit, for we could not have the desire for the Lord if the Spirit were absent. We must trust the presence of the Spirit within this desire and longing for the Lord and be willing to accept this prayer experience for as long as the Lord wills. The lessons contained in the experience of emptiness illuminate different aspects of our relationship to God, such as the meaning of being a creature and the necessity of the gift of his grace for all movement to him in prayer. It also deepens our faith by making us base it not on the presence of sensible consolations but at a much deeper level of our being.

Finally, and perhaps the hardest to recognize and accept, is the experience of desiring the Lord amid temptations, distractions, and boredom. On one level, we experience ourself as moving away from God because it seems that everything in us is moving just opposite of the desire to love and serve him. Yet amid these distractions we manage to cry out to the Lord to come and take these away and draw us closer to himself. We long for the time when the Lord was present with his consolations and peace. Yet we must recognize the presence of the Spirit even amid these tendencies of our nature. We could not have the desire for the Lord if the Spirit were absent. These experiences also illuminate an aspect of our relationship to God, that of a sinner needing ever more to be redeemed and helpless to do anything without God's help. These experiences, often referred to as "dark nights," are crucial for our growth in faith. Only in them do we discover whether we love the Lord of consolations or the consolations of the Lord. The fact that we cling to the Lord during these times of prayer and during these periods in our life is a more valid index of the depth of our faith relationship with him than the fact that we cling to him during sensible consolation.

Merton unequivocally presents the end of prayer as experienced communion with God. He asserts that the communion we seek in prayer is a "conscious realization of the union that is already effected between our souls and God by grace."[9] The immediate end of prayer may vary from asking God for help to giving God thanks for blessings. But the immediate end is not the ultimate end.

> . . . the ultimate end of all mental prayer is communion with God. Of course it is quite true that meditation disposes us for an immediate practical end on earth, with a view to our future union with God in heaven. But what I mean to emphasize here is that every meditation, every act of mental prayer, even if it may have some immediate practical purpose, should also bring us into direct

communion with God. This is the true fruit of meditation. Every
other immediate practical purpose is secondary and subordinate
to this one principle and all important end.[10]

In his later years Merton stopped using the terms *meditation*
and *mental prayer*. He felt their connotations were primarily intellectual and gave the wrong impression of what prayer really was. He
began speaking instead of "prayer of the heart," feeling that in the
English language the word *heart* came the closest to expressing the
center of our being from which flow our deepest human experiences,
including prayer.

> In the "prayer of the heart" we seek first of all the deepest ground
> of our identity in God. We do not seek to reason about dogmas of
> faith or the mysteries. We seek rather to gain a direct existential
> grasp, a personal experience of the deepest truths of life and faith,
> *finding* ourselves in God's truth.[11]

In Merton, contemplation is often used to describe the advanced level of prayer. Its purpose is the same as all prayer.

> . . . contemplation reaches out to the knowledge and even to the
> experience of the transcendent and inexpressible God. It knows
> God by seeming to touch him. Or rather it knows him as if it had
> been invisibly touched by him. . . . Touched by him who has no
> hands, but who is pure Reality and the source of all that is real!
> Hence contemplation is a sudden fit of awareness, the existential
> contact of which we speak when we use the metaphor of being
> "touched by God."[12]

And Merton reminds us that this experience of the Lord is the result,
not of our own efforts, but of the action of the Holy Spirit.

> He [the Holy Spirit] not only makes us understand something of
> God's love as it is manifested to us in Christ, but he also makes us
> live by that love and experience its action in our hearts. When we
> do so, the Spirit lets us know that this life and action are the life
> and action of Christ in us. And so the charity that is poured forth
> in our hearts by the Holy Spirit brings us into an intimate, experi-

ential communion with Christ. It is only by the Holy Spirit that we truly know and love Jesus and come through him to the knowledge and love of the Father.[13]

Prayer as the Discovery of God in the Depths of the Self

In prayer we seek communion with God; so, we must seek God where God is. And where on earth is the Lord primarily present? The New Testament tells us that since the resurrection and the sending of the Spirit, the Lord is present primarily in the hearts of believers. Our self-in-God model of the person is based on the truth. It should be quickly added that the fact of God's immanence in us in no way denies the truth of his transcendence. God's existence is not co-extensive with God's presence in people; God exists outside of us and before us from all eternity. But for our understanding of personal prayer it is important to recognize the complementarity between God's immanence and transcendence. Ordinarily we reach the transcendent Lord outside ourselves by first discovering the Lord within ourselves. The beginning of prayer is the discovery of the God-with-us and not the God-out-there.

I don't believe that this truth has been adequately acknowledged in our past approaches to personal prayer. Reflecting on my own experience I can see two main reasons for this. First, our spirituality was based on a self-outside-God model. We felt that God existed primarily in heaven. The purpose of spirituality was to bridge the gap between God and ourselves. Prayer was crucial in this effort; we called out and hoped he would hear and come down to help us. Prayer was basically our effort to reach him. I believe that the second reason that the immanence of God was not adequately acknowledged as the starting point for prayer was the essentially negative and distrustful attitude we had to human nature. We focused more on our sinfulness than on our redemption. Hence, if we entered deeply into ourselves, we would find mainly tendencies to evil, and surely this was no starting point for prayer! We were convinced that sin in us was more powerful than grace in us, and so we could not trust the Spirit to bring us to the Lord. The alternative was to build a bridge by our own effort, struggling with great intellectual effort to conquer our distractions and direct some appropriate thoughts and desires to the Lord.

Over and over Merton emphasizes the truth that we cannot discover our true selves without simultaneously discovering the Lord. If we have not found him in ourselves, we do not know ourselves: "Our desire and our prayer should be summed up in St. Augustine's words: *Noverim te; noverim me* (May I know you, may I know myself)."[14]

> ... whatever is in God is really identical with him, for his infinite simplicity admits to no division and no distinction. Therefore I cannot hope to find myself anywhere except in him. Ultimately the only way that I can be myself is to become identified with him in whom is hidden the reason and fulfillment of my existence. Therefore there is only one problem in which all my existence, my peace and my happiness depend: to discover myself in discovering God. If I find him, I will find myself, and if I find my true self, I will find him.[15]

But, Merton quickly adds, we do not discover God; God discovers us. All our approaches to him depend on his drawing us to himself.

> Our discovery of God is, in a way, God's discovery of us. We cannot go to heaven to find him because we have no way of knowing where heaven is or what it is. He comes down from heaven and finds us. He looks at us from the depths of his own infinite actuality, which is everywhere, and his seeing us gives us a new being and a new mind in which we also discover him. We only know him insofar as we are known by him. . . .[16]

Merton points out that entering into our true selves is not simply introspection; we look within ourselves to pass beyond self: "At that moment the point of our contact with him opens out and we pass through the center of our own nothingness and enter into infinite reality, where we awaken as our true self."[17] And again: ". . . it is by the door of this deep self that we enter into the spiritual knowledge of God. (And, indeed, if we see our true selves it is not in order to contemplate ourselves but to pass beyond ourselves and find him.)"[18]

And Merton sees prayer at the heart of the process of entering our true selves and opening to the presence of God at our depths.

> That is what prayer is all about. Prayer is not really just a way of addressing God out there somewhere. Prayer is opening up this deepest conscience and consciousness, a mystical conscience and a mystical consciousness, in which God and I work together. It is not merely a faculty of my psychological being. The problem is that we do not have a theological ideal of man, and even today—perhaps especially today—much of the new thinking about man and about prayer is confused and confusing because it starts from a totally different concept of conscience and consciousness.[19]

He repeated the same truth in the last talk he gave on prayer in the United States, before he left on his journey to Asia.

> In prayer we discover what we already have. You start where you are and you deepen what you already have, and you realize that you are already there. We already have everything; but we don't know it and we don't experience it. Everything has been given to us in Christ. All we need is to experience what we already possess.[20]

Prayer as Resting in the Lord

We have been understanding prayer as the expression of our relationship to the Lord under the influence of the Holy Spirit. Throughout the emphasis has been on recognizing the centrality of the Spirit in enabling us to move to the Lord in prayer. A final truth should be emphasized because it has not been adequately stressed in the past: the movement of our personal prayer will generally be toward less activity on our part and more activity on the Spirit's part. This movement of the Spirit will not be marked by a great deal of intellectual activity but by a quiet resting in the presence of the Lord. As in human relationships, words become less necessary the more we get to know a person; good friends can enjoy one another's company while saying very little. This is also true for our relationship with the Lord. It should be quickly added, however, that the Holy Spirit will not always be moving us to rest passively in the Lord. We may have been moved to pour out our feelings in love, to recite a psalm, to sing a song. The important principle is that what we do in prayer we do in response to the prompting of the Spirit. But we must firmly believe that the Spirit is also working in us when we feel moved just to sit quietly in the Lord's presence saying nothing of much consequence but knowing the Lord is there.

Merton points out that not understanding this dynamic of the Spirit has caused many people to interfere with the simple movement of prayer by substituting a rather compulsive routine of intellectual activity.

> If on the other hand we speak of meditation as "mental prayer," consisting of busy discursive acts, complex logical reasoning, active imagining and the deliberate stirring up of affections, then we find, as St. John of the Cross shows, that this kind of meditation tends to conflict with our silent and receptive attention to the inner working of the Holy Spirit, especially if we attempt to carry on with it once its usefulness has come to an end. Misplaced effort in the spiritual life often consists in stubbornly insisting upon compulsive routines which seem to us to be necessary because they accord with our own short-sighted notions.[21]

And in his later years Merton moved away from talking about "mental prayer" with all its implications of intellectual busyness. He talked of "prayer of the heart," which did not carry these implications.

> The prayer of the heart introduces us into deep interior silence so that we learn to experience its power. For that reason prayer of the heart has to be always very simple, confined to the simplest acts and often making use of no words or thoughts at all.[22]

This silence cannot be forced, and the amount of activity on our part will surely vary. Beginners in prayer will have to do more than those more advanced. Those more advanced will need more activity on certain days, depending on the need of the day and the amount of distractions. In general, if we sense that the intellectual activity is helpful in drawing us closer to the Lord, then it should be used. Normally more will be present during the opening periods of prayer than during the final periods. Usually it is a matter of allowing the Spirit to lead us through this activity to a quiet resting in the Lord.

Merton is comfortable describing prayer as resting in the Lord. The following statement, appearing in his final book on prayer, sums this up; it applies to all who take prayer seriously, not simply to monks for whom the book happened to be written.

> Hence monastic prayer, especially meditation and contemplative prayer, is not so much a way to find God as a way of resting in him whom we have *found*, who loves us, who is near to us, who comes to us to draw us to himself. *Dominus enim prope est.*[23]

He assures us that within this rest a great deal is going on.

> The absence of activity in contemplative prayer is only apparent. Below the surface, the mind and will are drawn into the orbit of an activity that is deep and intense and supernatural, and which overflows into our whole being and brings forth incalculable fruits.[24]

Merton quotes a medieval spiritual writer to summarize his point: "God works in us while we rest in him." His own words bring together his thought on the experience of those who are growing in the practice of prayer.

> Contemplative prayer is a deep and simplified spiritual activity in which the mind and will rest in a unified and simple concentration upon God, turned to him, intent upon him and absorbed in his own light, with a simple gaze which is perfect adoration because it silently tells God that we have left everything else and desire even to leave our own selves for his sake, and that he alone is important to us, he alone is our desire and our life, and nothing else can give us any joy.[25]

Praying Always

Our considerations have focused on formal prayer, on the times that we withdraw from our activities to be alone with the Lord. This could leave the impression that our spontaneous prayers to the Lord are not as important. Almost all we have considered about prayer relates very easily to the prayers that arise in our hearts during our daily activities. When Paul encourages us to "pray always," he does not intend that we withdraw from activity; he surely didn't, nor did Jesus. But he does mean that we allow the Spirit to express our relationship to the Lord frequently during the day. For the Spirit that joins It's voice to ours during formal prayer will also join us in our informal prayer. There can be no better preparation for our times of being alone in prayer with the Lord than a dialogue during the day in which we remain aware of the Lord during our activities.

REFLECTION QUESTIONS

1. List attitudes to personal prayer you have noticed in yourself and others that flow predominantly from a self-outside-God understanding of prayer.

2. Describe experiences from recent prayer in which you recognized the power of the Spirit at work. What signs helped you recognize the Spirit?

3. Have you had experiences in prayer in which God seemed absent, though your desire for him remained? Explain.

4. Describe an experience from recent prayer in which you seemed unable to yield to the movement of the Spirit and seemed more drawn toward temptations and distractions. Were you praying? Explain.

5. Describe how your understanding of personal prayer has developed over the years. Compare and contrast your present understanding with the one presented here.

IV IMPROVING PERSONAL PRAYER

I have been describing personal prayer as the expression of our relationship to God under the influence of the Holy Spirit. To improve the quality of our expressions two things are implied in the definition: first, that we improve the relationship in general; and second, that we use methods that can yield ever more to the influence of the Spirit. I will now reflect on the practical ways of improving prayer by improving our relationship with God outside of prayer and by improving our ability to respond to the Spirit during prayer. I will then discuss the most effective ways to use the word of God as a starting point for prayer and the general reasons why at times it seems we are unable to pray. Again, I am concerned primarily with personal prayer made during the times of withdrawal from activity. This is in no way undermining the importance of continually expressing our relationship to God during activity. It will become clear during our discussion how intimately related are the two types of prayer.

Improving Our Relationship with God

Since prayer is the expression of our relationship with God, it will always reflect the quality of this relationship. In short, if we want to improve our prayer, we must first improve our relationship. I believe that many of us entertain a false assumption that improving prayer is primarily a matter of learning the right techniques and methods. Then we give these new techniques and methods a try and find that not much happens. But prayer is not much different from human friendships. The expressions we receive from our friends are as valuable to us as the depth of the relationship which supports them. We are immediately wary of glowing expressions of love and concern that never flow into actions. So also with the Lord. Our words to him in prayer are as valuable as our habitual relationship with him. Unfortunately there are no tricks or short cuts, and we ought not to expect some particular method to compensate for an indifferent or lukewarm relationship. Jesus put the matter in terms of our heart: "For where your treasure is, there will your heart be also" (Mt. 6:21). If our treasure is truly in the Lord and in loving and serving others for God's sake, then our heart will habitually seek this treasure. It will seek this treasure all the day long; it will seek this treasure in prayer. Jesus himself gave a good example of the quality of heart supporting prayer. He was stopped in the middle of a busy day preaching to the crowds and asked by one of his disciples how to pray. Jesus was able to teach them to pray by articulating the quality of his own heart at the time: "Father, hallowed be thy name; thy kingdom come; thy will be done."

The goal of Christian life is to live with this habitual quality of heart; if we do this, we will have no trouble praying. Our expressions to God will be as natural and spontaneous as our expressions to our friends. But the problem is that we cannot achieve this quality of heart by ourselves. It is the result of our cooperation with the work of the Spirit in us. The Spirit in us is always impelling us to love and serve God and others and to move beyond merely self-centered concerns. Paul puts it succinctly:

> Let me put it like this: if you are guided by the Spirit you will be in no danger of yielding to self-indulgence, since self-indulgence is the opposite of the Spirit; the Spirit is totally against such a thing, and it is precisely because the two are so opposed that you do not always carry out your good intentions (Gal. 5:16–17).

The tension in our lives is always between love and selfishness. To improve our relationship with God, we need to yield our hearts more and more to the Spirit who directs us always beyond ourselves to God and others. If we do this, prayer—both formal and spontaneous—becomes a natural expression of our habitual quality of heart.

Discovering Obstacles to the Spirit

The biggest problem in improving our relationship with the Lord is discovering the many different ways in which our hearts are directed primarily toward our own interests and only secondarily, or not at all, toward the Lord's service. The discovery of these obstacles to the Spirit demands a continual awareness of the motivation underlying our daily activities. Often we are unaware of our true motivation; it takes a great deal of reflection to discover it. We may find that what we presumed we were doing for the Lord's service we were really doing for ourselves. It is really not too difficult to discover the very obvious ways we block the Spirit's work. These stand out in certain relationships with others that are marked by pettiness, jealousy, lust, dislike, even hatred. Inordinate attachments to worldly things such as money, power, and prestige also stand out. In all these, our hearts do not seek God's kingdom and we know it. But I don't believe that this level of obvious sinful tendencies is the major barrier in improving our general relationship to the Lord.

Another level of motivation which we never put in the realm of sin but which, nevertheless, is not in tune with the Spirit can habitually dominate our lives. At this level, our hearts are truly on ourselves, but we do not know it. I believe that for many conscientious Christians this becomes the major obstacle in relating to the Lord. For many of us the cutting-edge of the growth of our relationship to God, and simultaneously of our prayer, comes in discovering these very subtle obstacles to the Holy Spirit. We all have our own particular pattern of obstacles to the Spirit related to our personality and our vocation in life. As I look back over my years of teaching, I can discern a series of rather subtle obstacles which dominated my motivation at the time, often without my knowledge. I believe I was living a good life, and that I was, in general, directed by the Spirit. However, I believe that becoming aware of these less obvious obstacles and then bringing them to the Lord had much to do with establishing a deeper sense of the Lord's presence in my everyday life, enhancing my relationship with the Lord and also my prayer.

In the first two years of teaching I experienced a great deal of anxiety, stemming mainly from my feeling of incompetence. I habitually compared myself to other teachers and saw them far ahead of me. To compensate I would try very hard to do well in the classroom, with the hope that students would begin to acknowledge me as a qualified teacher. I was habitually aware of how well or poorly each class went and worried from one class to the next. In this subtle way I was focused a great deal of the time on myself; I wanted to do well for my own sake rather than to serve the Lord and others better. I can recall very gradually getting over these feelings of anxiety. Beginning to get a reputation as a good teacher, I was gaining confidence in myself. A great deal of my anxiety disappeared. In comparing myself with my colleagues, I found that I was doing as well and even better than they. I recall entering the classroom with an entirely different attitude. Now I was no longer anxious lest I do a poor job and get a bad reputation; I was eager to go in, present my matter, and wait for the students to respond enthusiastically. But in a very subtle way I wanted to do well not primarily to love and serve the students better but to gain a reputation for myself. In short, I was becoming proud and increasingly dominated by a desire for prestige among students and faculty. I was building my kingdom, not the Lord's. Since so much of my life centered upon my work of teaching, this habitual pattern of subtle self-seeking would be present throughout the day, undermining my response to the Spirit and total service to the Lord.

I then experienced a different pattern of obstacles to the Spirit. As I became more effective, my reputation spread and I became more in demand for extra classes, talks, and presentations both at the university and in the community. At first I responded enthusiastically, rather pleased with my growing success. But I gradually discovered that in doing this I had to sacrifice time I previously had available to pursue my own personal interests, both in work and in relaxation. The excitement wore off and I began to feel sorry for myself because I had so little time for myself. This led to a pattern of self-pity: why should I have to do so much more than others? Again, in a very subtle way I was not responding to the Spirit but was focused upon myself; I was performing these activities but not always filled with the desire to love and serve the Lord through them. I subtly resented having to do them. About this time another obstacle arose. My entire day and most of my weekends were filled with work. I performed the work and finished all I committed myself to do. But at the end of the day I would feel empty. Rushing around, responding to all the requests and demands made of me, but not doing them with a heart full of the desire to do these jobs for the love of God, I was an empty man doing good deeds. I had allowed the pace of my life to develop in such a way that I did not allow myself time to regain the strength needed to serve the Lord wholeheartedly, the strength that comes from living in tune with the Spirit.

It soon became clear to me that these patterns in my life were not entirely good and were not promoting my relationship with the Lord. I don't want to over-exaggerate this because I believe I was leading a very good life and doing much under the influence of the Spirit. But these obstacles were also present and hurting the service in a subtle way. It became clear to me that these patterns, especially the last one, were undermining my relationship to the Lord in prayer. There was little I could do during the time of prayer to offset the habitual hurriedness of my life-pattern. I found it very difficult to quiet down, focus on the Lord, and allow the Spirit to unite us. Ironically, I was teaching courses on prayer all the while and presenting practical methods for praying with the implication that these would be effective in prayer irrespective of the quality of daily life. I became aware that this was not working in my own life and acknowledged that my great personal need was not for a new method to improve my prayer but for a rhythm of life that enabled me to live in tune with the Spirit. I recall switching the emphasis in my prayer courses from concern with proper methods to be used during prayer to concern with habitual openness to the Spirit outside of prayer. I learned that if my heart were dominated by the Spirit during my daily activities, my heart would be dominated by the Spirit during prayer. In the Lord's words, my heart would seek the Lord as its treasure during prayer to the degree it seeks the Lord as its treasure outside of prayer. I am not saying that activity in itself is an obstacle to prayer, but only that activity not in tune with the Spirit is destructive to prayer. Activity in tune with the Spirit is the best possible preparation for personal prayer.

There are two important corollaries. The first is that the discovery and naming of the obstacles to the Spirit make up the initial, though perhaps the hardest, step of the process: self-knowledge is often long in coming. After we have discovered them, we must wait patiently for the Lord to remove them; we cannot overcome our own selfishness without the Spirit. The second corollary is that, in order to discover our patterns of obstacles to the Spirit, we must first develop a rhythm of life that facilitates living in tune with the Spirit and recognizing which motivations in us flow from the Spirit and which do not. This lifestyle has many facets which we will discuss in detail in the next chapter. For now it is enough to name a few: adequate rest, recreation and exercise, time for quiet and reflection, personal prayer, liturgy, and examination of conscience. Examination of conscience is the crux of becoming aware of our habitual motivation; it is at the heart of improving our responsiveness to the Spirit in daily life. During these examinations we explicitly review our daily activities to see whether they have been directed to love and service of the Lord or merely to our own interests. Since the quality of our prayer is directly related to the quality of our daily activities, we can see how important is the regular daily practice of examination. The goal in establishing all these rhythms in our life is to live more in tune with the Holy Spirit. Our distant goal is to develop hearts like Christ's so that we could be stopped in the middle of our busiest day and express the same quality of heart that he expressed: "Father, hallowed be thy name; thy kingdom come; thy will be done."

Improving Our Response to the Spirit during Prayer

The second means for improving personal prayer is improving our response to the Spirit during the time of prayer. In stressing the role of the Spirit in prayer, there is a danger of undercutting the importance of our own role. What we do during prayer time is extremely important, for it can either facilitate or block the movement of the Spirit. God's Spirit joins our spirit; it does not replace it. In the final analysis, prayer is a cooperative venture between the Spirit and ourselves. Our role is to establish the proper conditions to foster attentiveness to the Spirit; the Spirit's role is to unite us to the Lord within these conditions. It should be recalled that we are now talking about the type of personal prayer that we make when we withdraw from activity to be with the Lord and not about our spontaneous prayers to the Lord during the day. It need only be pointed out that if we have been spontaneously relating to the Lord during the day, there will be no trouble in relating to the Lord in prayer. Let us slightly expand our previous definition of prayer in order to relate it more directly to these times of formal prayer. We will consider prayer now as the expression of our relationship to the Lord under the influence of the Spirit in response to the word of God. The key addition is "response to the word of God." Formal prayer then becomes the time of focusing on God's word and of allowing the Spirit to move our hearts in response to the word. The meaning of God's word here is very broad. I see it as containing at least four dimensions: the word of God in the sacraments, in Scripture, in the events of our life, in creation. In short, the starting point for prayer can be any aspect of the word of God: sacramental, scriptural, existential, created. Since we are discussing personal prayer and not liturgical prayer, we will talk only of the last three dimensions of the word of God.

The method I am presenting here is the one that I have found most helpful personally and also most helpful for my students. It is very general, but I believe that the more particular methods can easily be subsumed under it. In many cases I have found that the more detailed methods have been barriers rather than helps to the Spirit during prayer; we simply become over-concerned with using the method well, and this becomes a distraction to our attentiveness to the Spirit. We are focused on what we are doing. The goal of this method is to focus on the word of God in a way that our response to it comes under the influence of the Spirit. Our activity is to select the aspect of God's word to which we seem to be drawn on a particular day and then use our bodies and minds in a way that facilitates listening for the movements of the Spirit in our hearts. The goal is, of course, to allow the words, images, thoughts, and feelings that come only from ourselves to recede and to allow those which flow from the Spirit to replace them. A pre-condition for the use of this method is the acceptance of the self-in-God model of spirituality and a firm conviction that the Spirit will, indeed, unite our hearts to the Lord in response to God's word if we allow this. In short, we must trust the Spirit to unite us with Jesus and the Father, just as he united Jesus with the Father: that we may experience our oneness.

Using Our Bodies: Two Steps

How, then, should we use our bodies to foster attentiveness to the movements of the Spirit during prayer? We must choose an appropriate place and posture for prayer. First, we must choose a place in which we can be attentive to the word for a long period of time without distraction or fear of distraction. The atmosphere must be totally conducive to interior quiet. For me this means leaving my office. The atmosphere is distracting. If I am not actually interrupted by a phone call or a visitor, I fear that I will be and that the footsteps outside the door may be coming for me. In addition, in my office I am continually distracted by all the work I have yet to do. I find myself planning my activity after prayer. These subtle distractions interrupt my attentiveness to the Spirit. For me the best place to pray is in the chapel or in my bedroom. When I'm in the chapel or my bedroom, I am not distracted by anyone, nor do I fear that I will be. But at certain times I prefer to pray elsewhere. I can also pray sitting or walking in the garden. I have come to identify these three places with prayer, and I am cast into the mood of prayer when I go to them. Their general atmosphere facilitates interior quiet for me immediately.

Second, we must choose a posture which enables us to focus on the word of God for a long period without in itself becoming a distraction. The posture can become a distraction in two ways: both by being too comfortable, encouraging us to rest if not sleep, and by being too uncomfortable, drawing our attention away from the word of God to our discomfort. The general norm for most people is that the back be kept erect during prayer. For Christians this usually means sitting or kneeling. The Hindu yogi prefers a lotus position; the Buddhist monk prefers the squatting position with a small pillow. In all cases the back is erect. The position must reflect the importance attached to the activity of prayer. Prayer is our opening to our God. Everything about our posture should be conducive both to attention and to reverence. I prefer the sitting position. I choose an ordinary simple chair that is slightly padded in the seat and on the back and that will support me in an erect sitting position. I find that in this position I can sit erect for thirty minutes without relaxing too much and without developing any aches in my body. I let my arms fall naturally from my shoulders and rest my hands, palms up, on my lap. I keep my feet flat on the floor about a foot apart; crossing my legs usually makes me a bit too comfortable and therefore less attentive. I tilt my head slightly forward and close my eyes. Some find it more helpful to keep their eyes open and to focus on a spot on the floor several feet in front of them.

There are days when I cannot relax enough to take this posture. I then usually decide to use a slightly more relaxed position or to walk in the garden. But if I am walking, it is important to try to be just as attentive to the word of God. For me this means walking slowly with eyes focused a few feet in front of me. Walking casually around outside, looking around at the flowers and birds, is a very good way for me to relax, but it is not a good way to be attentive to the Spirit speaking through God's word. The Lord's movements in our hearts are very subtle, and they can be ignored easily. Everything we do with our bodies should be conducive to attentiveness. This is in no way denying the value of casual walking and chatting with the Lord. Walking in the garden and praising God for the beauty in creation is surely a good type of prayer. On certain days it may even be the appropriate type for ourselves. But I don't believe it should become normative. The Christian tradition, reinforced by all religious traditions, teaches us that the deepest prayer to the Lord will occur when we remove ourselves from all distractions and focus totally on God's word so that the Spirit can move in our hearts in response to it.

Using Our Minds: Five Steps

Our role in prayer is providing the conditions in which we can be attentive to the movements of the Spirit in us. The first set of conditions relate to an appropriate use of our bodies; the second set of conditions concern the appropriate use of our minds, our mental activities. How, then, can we use our minds to bring our words, thoughts, and feelings more and more under the influence of the Spirit? The general method I have found most helpful personally contains five steps: quieting down, making acts of the presence of God, focusing on the word of God, listening and responding to the word, and concluding with a short prayer. First, at the opening of our prayer we must relax and quiet down. It helps if before beginning the prayer period itself we begin slowing down our activities and recalling what we are about to do. This, plus the general atmosphere of the place where we are accustomed to pray daily, may put us immediately in a quiet, relaxed state, ready to pray. The quieting down is not really prayer; it is getting our minds ready to begin praying. If we are praying early in the morning soon after we get up, our minds may not yet be preoccupied with the worries of the day, and we may become quiet almost immediately. However, if we are upset because of disturbing dreams during the night, we may have to reflect briefly on these before we can settle down. If we make our prayer later in the day after we have been working, it may take longer to put these distractions aside and become aware of what we are about to do. We must put our anxieties in his hands and begin to relax in his presence. Breathing deeply and rhythmically and focusing attention on different areas of the body are two common ways to foster relaxation. I find there are times when I am immediately relaxed in the presence of God and ready to pray, and other times when I don't seem to become relaxed and present during the entire period because I am so anxious about my own problems. At these times I find it most helpful just to begin reading a psalm, repeat a favorite Scripture passage over and over, or say the Our Father slowly. There have been periods in which I have not been able to quiet down for days. In general, I find it best to pray early in the day, after getting up but before breakfast.

The second step is making appropriate acts of the presence of God. As we gradually become quiet, we get an increased realization of what we are about to do, and almost spontaneously we move toward expressing ourselves to God in acts of humility, reverence, love, and petition for help. We realize that all movement toward God during prayer depends on the work of the Spirit, and we ask God to send the Spirit. We realize that we are often unfaithful in serving God and unworthy to be with God but recall that God loves us, forgives our sins, and wants to be with us even more than we want to be with God, and we make acts of thanks for this love. These acts will rise spontaneously within us; there is no set pattern. They will differ from day to day depending on our mood. We are now praying because we are expressing our relationship to God; the Holy Spirit is already at work.

It is important that we be patient with these opening stages of prayer. A quiet, subtle process is involved in coming into the presence of God that cannot be rushed, very much like coming into the presence of a friend. We often short-circuit this process. Rather than slowly quieting down and letting appropriate acts emerge from where we truly are, we begin a constant stream of conversation that flows from a rather superficial level of our being. We erroneously identify our prayer with this conversational chatter and feel that we have begun to pray when we have merely begun a stream of conversation that may be rather compulsive. We have begun to pray when we have allowed the Spirit to move us; this may or may not involve many words.

The third step in using our minds to facilitate the work of the Spirit is focusing on the word of God. We must direct our attention to the word of God in a way that permits the Spirit to move in us in response to this word. A caution is in order. If we find that during the quieting down process and opening acts of prayer our hearts are already moving easily and spontaneously toward the Lord and that a sense of the Lord's presence is emerging, we should not move on. There is no necessity to move toward focusing on a different aspect of the word of God when the Spirit has already united us with the Lord, which is, after all, the goal of prayer. We may find that we are before the Lord in great gratitude, and we express this in words or silence. Or we may find that we are before God in great need—as was Jesus in Gethsemane—and we express this. Or we may simply be aware of God's presence, content just to be there without making any special acts of praise or petitions. So we remain in this presence, ready to spend the remainder of the prayer time here. However, if our hearts do not seem to be moving easily toward the Lord at this point, then we begin our focusing on the word of God we have chosen beforehand. We ought to choose that aspect of the word which best expresses where we think we are before God. This may be an important event from the day or a Scripture passage that is currently significant for us. The best place to begin prayer is where we truly are. Beginning here we remain open so that the Spirit can draw us to God as It wills. As we focus on the word we have chosen, we may find our hearts subtly drawn in a different direction, and we must yield to this direction. Jesus gives an example of this prayer in

Gethsemane; he begins by praying that the cup he has been asked to drink be removed and ends by reaffirming the deepest desire in him, that his Father's will be done. We must always be open to be drawn from where we are to where the Lord wants us to be. In my personal experience, something from my life usually emerges during the opening of prayer, and I focus upon it. This may vary from gratitude for a good class I gave to petition for help in dealing with a person I dislike. I find that a Scripture passage comes to mind that sums up where I am before the Lord and then I focus gently on the passage. I can then rest before the Lord; God's Spirit has joined mine and is uniting me with God.

The fourth step is waiting, listening, and responding to the word of God under the influence of the Spirit. We have chosen some aspect of God's word and are now quietly holding it before us, without straining. We do this by recalling the event, or by slowly repeating a short phrase or slowly rereading a short Scripture passage. We use our mental abilities to wait, listen, and be attentive to the Spirit's movements. We may initiate our own considerations, but we do this hesitantly, always ready to yield to the Spirit, should the Spirit move us in a different direction. The goal of our prayer is not to weave our own meditation around the word of God but to allow the Spirit to speak through the word and influence all our words, thoughts, and feelings. The biggest danger is impatience. We become uneasy with the quiet waiting in the presence of the Lord and decide to construct our own response to his word. We must be convinced that the Spirit in us will move us toward the Lord and learn to recognize the different types of experience which are signs of this movement. It is better to wait empty, open, and desiring the Lord's presence than to construct a superficial string of thoughts that are merely our own. However, as we wait patiently in the presence of the Lord, we may find that we are moved by the Spirit to speak, read Scripture, or recite a prayer. Then because we are responding to the Spirit, we continue to speak, read, or be silent, however we are moved: his spirit has joined our spirit.

The fifth and final step of this process is making an appropriate closing prayer. During the last few minutes of prayer we draw together where we are in the presence of the Lord and express this simply. We can also look ahead to our day and ask for the continued support of his presence. Many find the Our Father the perfect conclusion to the period of personal prayer since it commits us to leave prayer and begin working for the Father's kingdom. It is appropriate to be especially reverent during these minutes. But it is important to note that we should not close our prayer before the period we previously decided is over. It is the experience of most that the process I have described cannot be done effectively on a regular basis in less than twenty minutes; it takes time to quiet down and become sensitive to the Spirit's movements. A period of twenty to forty-five minutes is the most usual amount of time given to personal prayer. A daily rhythm of this sort is essential for most to foster a deepening relationship with the Lord in prayer and in service.

The Spirit and the Word of God

We have been understanding prayer as the expression of our relationship to God under the influence of the Holy Spirit in response to the word of God. This definition is based on the conviction that the Spirit of God will move our hearts in response to the word of God. Prayer time is simply a time of heightened sensitivity to the word, a sensitivity caused by allowing the Spirit to speak to us through God's word. It is important to point out the dangers involved in this understanding of prayer. There is the tendency in using the method we have given not to allow the Spirit to speak through the word but simply to construct our own meditation around the word.

I believe that this danger is most present in using the scriptural Word of God. We know that Scripture is a privileged place to meet the Lord. Isaiah gave the classic Old Testament expression of the power of the word.

> Yes, as the rain and the snow come down from the heavens and do not return without watering the earth, making it yield and giving growth to provide seed for the sower and bread for the eating, so the word that goes from my mouth does not return to me empty, without carrying out my will and succeeding in what it was sent to do (Is. 55:10–11).

The Epistle to the Hebrews expresses a similar theme.

> The word of God is something alive and active: it cuts like any double-edged sword but more finely: it can slip through the place where the soul is divided from the spirit, or joints from the marrow; it can judge the secret emotions and thoughts (Heb. 4:12).

The danger of blocking the action of the Spirit is very present in this type of meditation. Often we come to prayer with a pre-conceived goal in mind. We then select the passage of Scripture that deals with the goal and construct a stream of thoughts and images of Christ to reinforce this goal. It may be impossible for the Spirit to break through our activity. In the method we are suggesting we would read a Scripture passage slowly, reread it, then perhaps return to a word, phrase, or sentence which strikes us, focus upon this, and allow the Lord to move from here. The Spirit may move us in the direction we have chosen, or It may move in a different way. We must be open to this, recalling Paul's advice that often we do not know how to pray as we ought but that the Spirit in us will express our pleas to God according to God's will.

This danger is also present in using the existential word of God as our starting point for prayer. We know that God works in the world; God is a God of history. The Old Testament people continually praised the Lord for being active in leading them from Egypt to the promised land; we continually praise the Lord for being active in Jesus and in us. Perhaps the easiest way to pray is to begin with the awareness of how God is now working in our lives. In prayer we may focus on God's presence in some activity we've done or in some action of the Spirit in other people. I find it easy to praise the Lord for being active in me enabling me to give a good class, as well as for being active in students I teach who are eagerly striving to understand the theological truth I am presenting in class. I simply recall this activity of the Spirit, focus my attention gently upon it, and wait for the Spirit to unite me to the Lord in response to my attention. Gradually my own thoughts and considerations recede, and a new sense of God's presence emerges. I can then rest in this presence. But the ever-present danger is that I will simply begin reflecting on the happening by myself, putting together the various aspects of the experience, and asking why the particular class presentation was success-ful. My prayer can easily turn into a reflection on my life. While this reflection is good and very necessary, it is not the same as prayer. In it I am not allowing the Spirit to draw me to God; I am concerned more primarily with reviewing my own activities. This danger is most present if I begin prayer with a particular anxiety from my life that is unresolved and for which I need God's healing and grace. Rather than focusing quietly on my need for God, I can become all wrapped up in the problem itself and actually become more separated from God while focusing upon it. I may not be able to yield to the movement of the Spirit and allow the Spirit to strengthen me through a greater per-sonal experience of God as my Father and Jesus as my Savior.

This same danger can be present in using the created word of God as our starting point. We know that God created all things, sus-tains them in existence, and works through them to draw us to God. God's power and beauty are present around us in people and in cre-ation. In using this starting point we simply focus on the beauty of creation or the goodness of a person and allow the Spirit to draw us to the Lord through a heightened awareness of God's presence in them. The danger is that we can remain intrigued with beauty in itself or warmed by the recollection of a friend in a way that does not bring us to the Lord. We don't move from creation to the Creator. Rather than waiting quietly and attentively in the presence of the cre-ated word of God, we begin our own string of reflections, which may be an obstacle to the work of the Spirit.

Even though the existential and the created word of God can become an obstacle to the Spirit, I feel that we do not use them often enough as starting points for our prayer. We seem more comfortable using Scripture. I find that starting my prayer by focusing upon God's presence in events, people, and creation is more effective than starting with Scripture. The following dynamic is often present in my prayer. I quiet down and during my opening acts of prayer some blessing or problem emerges from the previous day. I then decide to use that for prayer, focusing upon it and asking the Lord to unite me to God through it. A quiet series of reflections often follows. My reflection recedes and often a short Scripture passage emerges which expresses perfectly where I am before the Lord. I then focus upon this passage, slowly repeating it. Gradually I may find it unnecessary to use the passage, and I rest quietly in the Lord's presence, often saying nothing. In this way I combine my own life situation with a passage of Scripture, and together the two lead me to a deeper awareness of my relationship with the Lord and may then yield to a quiet resting in God's presence.

Why We Can't Pray

Prayer should be a normal and natural expression of the most fundamental relationship in our lives, our relationship to God. As we grow in this relationship, expressing it in prayer becomes simpler and more fulfilling. But there are times when the relationship is very difficult to express, and it seems that we just cannot pray—the whole process is not that much different from expressing human relationships. There are many reasons for finding it difficult to pray. We often quickly conclude that we are using the wrong method and that finding a better one will automatically improve our prayer. Though an inappropriate use of a method is one reason we seem unable to pray, it is not the only reason—nor do I believe it is even the main reason.

I believe that the chief reason we find difficulty praying flows directly from the quality of our general relationship to the Lord. If our hearts are not primarily focused on loving and serving him but are primarily focused on serving our own interests, prayer is bound to be difficult. It will be difficult in direct proportion to our self-centeredness. The heart of a sinner does not seek the Lord during prayer any more than it seeks the Lord during activity. The sinful dimension in us may be great or small. In either case, it implies that there is an area of our life outside the influence of the Spirit. Complacently accepting any pattern of sin will affect prayer. God's Spirit cannot join our spirit and bring us to the Lord because we do not want to go to the Lord but prefer to remain fixed on serving ourselves. Since the Spirit in us is blocked from uniting us to God, we have to substitute our own activity. Prayer then becomes our monologue to God; we compose appropriate acts of worship that flow from a superficial level of our being. This is difficult because our expressions are often opposed to where we truly are: we tell the Lord we want to love and serve God in all, but we have just spent the day serving ourselves and perhaps even habitually offending God and others. Prayer will remain difficult until we acknowledge our need for conversion. If during the process of quieting down we become aware of the sinful obstacle within us and want to be healed from it, then the Spirit can continue working in us, uniting us to the Lord in sorrow and humility. And prayer becomes easier. Obviously it will be the conscious and willful dimension of sin that will be the greatest obstacle to prayer. But even the dimensions of self-centeredness of which we are unaware will hurt prayer because they hurt our general relationship to God. Much prayer will center around becoming aware of this sinfulness in us and bringing it to the Lord. The difficulty for prayer comes when we resist acknowledging it.

The second reason we have difficulty praying is that we are unable to quiet down enough to become sensitive to the movements of the Spirit. This usually happens because we have been living our lives at too fast a pace. Rushing from one activity to the next, we lose touch with the Spirit. We are not moving against the Spirit in a sinful way, but we are not allowing the Spirit to infuse our activities, enabling us to perform them in peace and joy. Finding ourselves anxious and worried both about the result of our work and about getting it all finished within the allotted time, we come to prayer restless and find it almost impossible to quiet our minds in a way that allows us to be sensitive to the movements of the Spirit. Since we cannot allow the Spirit to bring us to the Lord, we begin composing our own monologue to the Lord, expressing our own needs and concerns, often in a rushed and rather compulsive way. It often seems that we could be using our time more effectively by skipping prayer and finishing the work we left undone. Prayer will remain difficult until we develop a rhythm of life that enables us to work in tune with the Spirit, thus experiencing the peace and joy that flows from the Spirit's presence. If we are living in tune with the Spirit during the day, it is easy to allow the Spirit to unite us to the Lord during prayer.

I believe that deliberate sinfulness and the hurried pace of our lives are the two main reasons we find difficulty praying. But there are two other reasons; these are directly related to the method used during prayer. First, prayer is difficult when the method we use is not truly an authentic expression of our relationship to God. Many people have a very formalistic notion of prayer and feel compelled to go through routines they were taught. Neither the language nor the subject matter of their prayer flows naturally from their daily relationship to the Lord. The subject matter may be assigned either from Scripture or from a meditation book; the language is stilted and awkward. God's Spirit is not allowed to join their spirit and raise them to the Lord from the center of life. Prayer remains difficult until we are not afraid to be before the Lord where we truly are and then allow his Spirit to draw us from there. Second, prayer will also be difficult if we use methods inappropriate to our level of relationship to the Lord. Very commonly people who have been praying faithfully for a long time feel that they have to continue making frequent acts of the intellect and will, even though the Spirit may be moving them to rest in the Lord without saying much, or even anything at all. They may be resisting the movement of the Spirit and so find that prayer is becoming difficult and boring. On the other hand, those who are just beginning to make formal prayer regularly may try certain methods of prayer that are more appropriate for those advanced in prayer. Rather than continue to make the acts of intellect and will that help them express their relationship to God, they may try a method that involves very little thinking and wonder why they experience so many distractions.

I believe that these four reasons summarize some of the reasons we have difficulty praying. These difficulties are real, but I've also found that sometimes we say that we can't pray when we are actually praying quite well. We have a limited notion of the experiential signs of true prayer. Prayer is the movement of the Spirit at the deepest level of our being. As we have seen this movement resonates in a variety of ways in our consciousness: sensible consolation, quiet peace with little emotion but a deep faith conviction of God's presence, a desire for God who seems far away and even absent, a yearning for God amid desolation, boredom, distractions, and temptations. If we identify prayer only with the experience of sensible joy and consolation, it will often seem that we are not praying. This is not the truest sign of the movement of the Spirit in prayer. The most genuine sign is the desire for union with the Lord. If this desire is present, even though there are no joyful feelings—and even if we are full of distractions—the Spirit is working and we are praying. It is important that we acknowledge the Spirit's presence in these experiences and not allow ourselves to feel frustrated and discouraged because "we can't pray." We can expect our prayer to contain frequent experiences of emptiness and distractions and temptations. These are important moments in our growth in union with the Lord, for during these difficult times the Holy Spirit is working deep in our hearts, purifying us and preparing us for deeper union with the Lord.

Praying in the Spirit

We must be careful not to exaggerate the difficulty of praying well; we can all pray because we have all received the Spirit. It is not difficult to find a method that helps us become more sensitive to the movement of the Spirit in our prayer, nor is it difficult to learn to recognize and respond to this movement. As we become sensitive to the Spirit's movements in our hearts during formal prayer, we become increasingly sensitive to the Spirit's movements in us during the day, and so our hearts spontaneously rise to God in informal prayer throughout the day. We find that without undue strain we are moving closer to fulfilling Paul's injunction to us to "pray always." The most comforting fact about the whole process is that we need not worry about "spiritual growth." We need only build rhythms into our lives that enable us to live in tune with the Spirit; the Spirit then does the rest, drawing us closer to the Lord both in prayer and in service. We will now look at some of the practical rhythms that help make us more sensitive to this work of the Spirit.

REFLECTION QUESTIONS

1. Describe the patterns in your daily life that seem to be the primary obstacles in your present relationship with God.

2. Describe the general method for the use of your body and mind that has been most helpful for your personal prayer. Compare and contrast your method with the one presented here.

3. Describe recent experiences of personal prayer illustrating each of the three starting points given: the scriptural word, the existential word, and the created Word.

4. Explain the chief reasons why you find prayer difficult and seem at times unable to pray. Compare and contrast these reasons with the ones presented here.

V GUIDELINES FOR LIVING IN THE SPIRIT

The danger in the presentation of the self-in-God model of spirituality is that it may seem too optimistic about human nature, leaving the impression that since we have all received the Spirit of Jesus, our sanctification is assured without much effort on our own part. This is assuredly a false impression. Growth in union with the Lord demands the total effort of our being. We have the challenge of arranging patterns in our life in such a way that we live in habitual contact with the Spirit and allow the Spirit to guide all our activities. The effort is difficult because of many pressures moving us away from the Spirit toward self-centered actions. Rather than respond to the Spirit we often find ourselves responding to these pressures. We don't have to be convinced of the pressures toward evil within ourselves. Daily we experience our self-centered drives for popularity, money, power, prestige, and pleasure; these can dominate our lives in very obvious ways and in very subtle ways, blocking our responsiveness to the Spirit. However, we are probably not fully aware of the pressure toward evil imposed on us from without. We are all products and victims of a culture which vaunts materialistic satisfaction as the chief means to happiness, continually reinforcing our internal tendencies toward selfishness. We see happiness as coming primarily from fulfilling all our personal needs and desires as much as possible. This self-centered orientation often puts us in conflict with other individuals, communities, and nations; any person, group, or nation that threatens this well-being becomes an enemy. The combination of our internal drive toward selfishness and the external pressures reinforcing this drive can motivate our life in a direction that is diametrically opposed to the message of the Gospel and the movement of the Holy Spirit.

The solution to this problem for us Christians is to build rhythms into daily life that foster living in tune with the Spirit and so counteract the evil which surrounds us. Just as we must provide the right conditions during prayer time to allow the Spirit to influence our movements to the Lord, so must we provide the right conditions during our daily life to allow the Spirit to direct all our motivations. The effort to provide conditions assuring our approach to the Lord in spite of pressures inside ourselves and in our society has traditionally been called asceticism. We will be considering asceticism, then, as our efforts with grace to build rhythms into our lives that foster living in tune with the Holy Spirit. We will discuss, first, some general criteria for a valid contemporary approach to asceticism, and, following this, some practical principles and practices for daily living in tune with the Spirit.

Criteria for Contemporary Asceticism

Before discussing the criteria for a contemporary asceticism, it is helpful to reflect on our previous approach. Too often in the recent past, asceticism has been identified with the efforts to control the evil tendencies which flowed from an essentially evil nature. Frequently we began with the assumption that, because of original sin, human nature has been damaged in such a way that it can never be trusted. We had a self-outside-God approach to spirituality, and not only were we outside God but our natures were fundamentally opposed to God. We were comfortable in locating most of the evil in our natures in our bodies; our bodies were separate from our souls and worked against them. The goal of asceticism was often seen as repressing, conquering, or controlling our evil bodies so that they might be more responsive to the demands of the soul. Ascetical practices often came to be identified with this self-denial. Lent was the period of self-denial: fast and abstinence was prescribed for adults; all were encouraged to give up some physical pleasure they enjoyed, such as candy, movies, cigarettes, or liquor. Today we cannot accept all the assumptions upon which this older approach was built. The self-in-God model of human nature insists that through our creation and our redemption, our natures are essentially good. It also insists that our bodies share in the goodness of this nature; they share in the effects of the redemption of Christ. Granted that tendencies to evil remain in us and are at times strong and very prevalent, still we know that through the grace of Christ we need not be dominated by them: grace is more powerful than sin. The effort of asceticism is not to repress our bodies but to bring all dimensions of our being, our bodies, minds, and spirits, under the influence of the Spirit of Christ.

There are two criteria for asceticism that I believe must be present today before contemporary Christians will take it seriously. First, it must be functional; it must clearly foster the goals of Christian living. In the past we were asked to perform certain practices that were not seen as fostering a better Christian life. For Catholics not eating meat on Friday was perhaps the most obvious. Today's asceticism must, then, be functional; it must foster becoming like Christ by living in tune with the Spirit. The Gospels present Jesus as totally dedicated to doing the Father's will in union with the Spirit. To be like Jesus, we too must always seek to know and to do the Father's will by allowing the Spirit to direct our lives. The practical challenge of asceticism will be to build rhythms in our daily life that enable us to live habitually in tune with the Spirit and so become like Jesus in knowing and doing the Father's will in love.

Practically this means that we must ask ourselves how God is calling us to love and serve him and his people; in other words, what is our vocation? And this question must be asked on two levels. First, what is the state in life God wants for me, and, second, how is he calling me on a day-to-day basis to fulfill this calling? Since the first question has been answered for most of us, the second question becomes the central one. For example, I believe that God has called me to be a Jesuit priest. The practical question I must ask is: how is he calling me to fulfill my vocation as a Jesuit priest each day? Since I am a theology teacher, this means that I must build rhythms into my life that insure I am in tune with the Spirit in my teaching, counseling, study, writing, and helping others. My challenge will be different from a housewife's or businessman's. But the goal for all of us is the same: to live in tune with the Spirit so that we can both know and do the Father's will in love each day. If I am successful in providing conditions in my daily life that facilitate the work of the Spirit, I can be sure that all my activities will be performed in love, that all my decisions will be made under the Spirit's guidance, and that my work will be done energetically and with enthusiasm in order the better to serve the God I love.

I have been stressing the fact that asceticism must be functional, related to doing God's will in tune with the Spirit. It is important to stress that this does not mean merely performing all our duties externally well. It means performing them with a quality of heart that reflects the presence of the Spirit. Paul gave us a list of those qualities that are signs of the Spirit's presence: love, joy, peace, patience, kindness, goodness, trustfulness, gentleness, and self-control. He also gave us a list of the qualities that are signs of the Spirit's absence: feuds, wrangling, jealousy, bad temper, quarrels, disagreements, factions, and envy. For me, the hardest challenge of asceticism is maintaining the quality of heart that reflects the Spirit's presence in the midst of the many activities, problems, and frustrations that make up my day. Most of us find it much easier simply to get our jobs done and not worry about our internal quality of heart—we all know the empty feeling of getting through a busy day and doing everything we were supposed to do but realizing that very little peace, love or joy was present. Though we have ostensibly done God's will, we have not really served God well; we have not lived in tune with the Spirit.

The second criterion for a valid contemporary asceticism is that it respect the total person: body, mind, and spirit. In the past the body was seen primarily as a barrier to life in the Spirit, the source of the evil in us and needing to be repressed. If asceticism is to regain its role in Christian living, it must clearly acknowledge the importance of the body and the crucial role it plays in our total service of the Lord. This is in no way to deny the continual inner tensions between the Spirit and our own selfish tendencies; if Paul was continually tormented by the tension, we surely should not expect to be free from it! We are only insisting that the body be respected as a part of the total person that has been redeemed by Christ. The good and evil in us flow from the three dimensions of our being working together: body, mind, and spirit. Our bodies and minds both serve crucial roles in the service of our spirits, the center of our love and freedom. How we use them will either help or hinder the openness of our spirit to God's Spirit. A valid contemporary asceticism must acknowledge the positive and vital role of both our bodies and minds in keeping us energetic in doing the Lord's will in tune with the Spirit.

Perhaps a note should be added on the importance of the psychological dimension, what we have been calling "the mind," for spiritual growth. It is clear how closely connected are psychological health and spiritual growth. God's Spirit joins our spirit and will be as effective in us as we permit him to be. This is obviously conditioned by the level of our personal maturity. One generally accepted touchstone of psychological maturity is the ability to make decisions without undue influence from pressures outside ourselves; decisions should flow from being in touch with an internal guiding principle. A growing body of knowledge from the social sciences shows how social structures affect our personal decisions without our being aware of them. These structures control the way we think and consequently the way we act. Many of these structures are opposed to the Gospel message; theologians today call these "sinful social structures." Examples frequently cited are attitudes and actions concerning private property, affluent life-style, sharing with the poor, war, nuclear weapons, and the environment. The majority of us fall into patterns of thinking on these issues that may be opposed to the Gospel message. A psychologically mature person will try to approach these areas openly and reach a decision in tune with personal internal principles; a less mature person will go uncritically along with the externally reinforced pattern of thinking and acting. The mature Christian is clearly called to make decisions in these areas flowing from the guidance of the Holy Spirit. This means stepping outside societal pressures. It is clear how this level of psychological freedom will directly influence a response to the Gospels. The conclusion for asceticism is that we must respect valid principles of both physical and psychological health in order that we may respond more fully and energetically to the movements of the Spirit in us. Thomas Merton expresses well the interaction of body, mind, and spirit that is a prerequisite for today's asceticism.

> The "spiritual life" is then the perfectly balanced life in which the body with its passions and instincts, the mind with its reasoning and its obedience to principle, and the spirit with its passive illumination by the light and love of God form one complete man

who is in God and with God and from God and for God. One
man in which God is all in all. One man in whom God carries out
his own will without obstacle.[1]

St. Paul puts it more simply: "Since the Spirit is our life, let us be
directed by the Spirit" (Gal. 5:25). We will now look at those practical principles and practices for the use of our bodies and minds that
help keep them responsive to the demands of the Spirit.

Practical Principles for Living in the Spirit: The Body

We have been understanding asceticism as our efforts with
grace to build rhythms into our daily lives that facilitate living in
tune with the Holy Spirit. These rhythms relate to the use of our
bodies, the use of our minds, and to our daily spiritual practices. We
will begin with the use of the body. The practical question is: What
rhythms are necessary in daily life to keep our bodies responsive to
the direction of the Spirit in energetically doing the Father's will?
There are two major principles: first, we must do whatever is necessary and possible to keep in good health and in good physical condition; and, second, we must do whatever is necessary to keep our
sensual desires responsive to the Spirit and not to our lower instincts,
that is, the part of our being that has not yet been transformed by the
Spirit. The first I am calling the positive principle for the use of the
body; the second, the negative principle. For me, the first is more important. It should be noted that the terms *body* and *mind* are being
used in a very general sense. All our actions are combinations of
body, mind, and spirit; it makes little sense to separate the different
functions, since they all work together. I am distinguishing them
only for the sake of discussion. I believe that the above principles are
applicable to everyone; however, how they are implemented will vary
greatly from person to person. The implementation must be related
to our unique personality characteristics and to our life situation.
What follows is a partial list of some of the rhythms I have found
helpful for myself in living in tune with the Spirit. Since my life-situation is not the ordinary one, these practices are listed only to give
examples of how I implement the general principles; they are not in-

tended to apply to anyone else as such. I am a forty-three year old Jesuit priest teaching theology at a midwestern Jesuit university.

To implement the first principle of keeping in good physical shape, I must build rhythms into my daily life that ensure I get enough exercise and enough rest. My work as a teacher does not involve much physical strain, nor am I by temperament inclined to seek exercise. Perhaps the greatest asceticism I practice is getting enough exercise to keep in shape and keep my weight down. Practically this means going to the university gym daily to jog or swim. I write these times into my schedule and, as far as possible, I am faithful to them. If I am regular in this exercise, my energy level remains high and I have more enthusiasm for my work; a beneficial side-effect is that many of the tensions that I have built up during the day are worked off through the exercise. So in addition to leaving the gym physically invigorated, I also leave more peaceful. To keep my body energetic in responding to the Spirit, I must also build into my schedule adequate time for sleep and rest. I need at least seven hours of sleep a night. Without this amount of sleep on a regular basis, I become tired during my activities. This leads to short-temperedness and a general lack of peace and love during my work. It is also helpful for me to take a thirty minute rest after lunch; unfortunately, my schedule doesn't usually permit this. Getting enough exercise and rest are very practical ascetical challenges for me. To do this I must take time from activities that I enjoy more or make time where seemingly none exists. The principles for exercise and rest are general principles and cannot be applied all the time. However I have found that I cannot neglect either adequate exercise or rest on a regular basis without seriously affecting my living in tune with the Spirit and so loving and serving the Lord energetically. When I have had enough exercise and rest, I find that I can work much more efficiently and effectively; in the long run I probably save time by taking time for these practices.

The negative principle of keeping my sensual instincts responsive to the Spirit and not my lower human nature also involves some regular practices for me. I enjoy food and have a tendency to eat and drink too much, especially if I'm anxious, tired, and not getting enough exercise. I can easily become dominated by this type of sensuality. To control myself I limit the amounts and kinds of food I eat to keep within a fixed weight level, a level apppropriate for my age and body structure and one at which I feel best physically. I also have a tendency to drink too much alcohol. So I have to set a limit on the number of drinks I have and be careful lest I fall into a pattern of drinking more and more. In addition to establishing norms of moderation for food and drink, it is helpful for me occasionally to give up entirely certain types of food and drink, especially when I seem to be becoming preoccupied with fulfillment on this level. This abstinence helps me to restore a balance in myself and to regain an equilibrium in which my sensual desires are more responsive to the Spirit. The Christian ascetical tradition also teaches us that it can be important to voluntarily give up types of food and drink for periods of time, even when our balance has not been upset, in order to increase the desire for spiritual fulfullment. I have not worked out adequate principles for myself in this area yet, though I believe it is important to do so.

Practical Principles: The Mind

Just as important as developing rhythms for the use of the body is developing rhythms for the use of the mind. I don't believe this area has been given the attention it deserves in the past, largely because we were focusing our attention on the evil tendencies inherent in the physical side of our being. The practical question in this area is: What rhythms are necessary to keep a quality of heart that reflects the presence of the Spirit through the signs of peace, love, and joy? There are two major principles: first, we must do whatever is necessary and possible to keep an internally peaceful state of mind; second, we must do whatever is necessary to keep our mental activities responsive to the Spirit and not our lower human nature, that part of us still outside the influence of the Spirit. The first I am calling the positive principle; the second, the negative principle. Again for myself in this area, the positive principle is more important. I believe that this area is even more important for living in tune with the Spirit than the previous area. If the absence of peace, love, and joy in our lives is an indication of the absence of the Spirit, we can appreciate the pervasiveness of this dimension in blocking the Spirit. It is unfortunate that we do not adequately recognize the obstacle to the Spirit that we place by the often rushed and anxious rhythm of our daily activities. I am giving the following practices only as an example of the general principles I am presenting. The examples apply as such only to myself, with my special life-situation and personality characteristics.

My greatest personal challenge in the entire area of asceticism is implementing the positive principle of maintaining a quality of heart during my activities that reflects the presence of the Spirit. Because of the type of person I am, I experience many, many barriers to personal peace. I am very busy and often take on more work than I should; consequently, I am habitually getting behind in my work and rushing to catch up. In addition, I am somewhat of a perfectionist; I am over-conscientious about the outcome of the work, worrying both whether I'll perform it successfully and whether I'll finish it in time. Also, I have a tendency to intellectualize my life and not live in tune with my feelings; thus, I find it easy to block this dimension from awareness and do my work unaware of being peaceful, patient, and loving or impatient, rushing, and worrying. All three of these characteristics, either working alone or together, tend to keep me tense and alienated from my inner self and the Spirit. To counteract these tendencies, I must build rhythms in my daily life to put me in touch with the Spirit and ensure a quality of heart which reflects this presence through the peace and love I show during my activities. My basic approach to doing this is to build times in my day for being quiet and alone, away from my work and from people.

I've found three rhythms of quiet and relaxation that help me. First, it is important for me to be alone and quiet with no other intellectual task to do, just letting my mind unwind and allowing feelings, anxieties, and thoughts to bubble up from my depths so that I can be more aware of my real inner moods. I will stop frequently during the day during my activities to do this, especially when I notice that I am getting tense. I will also pause shortly before beginning a major activity, such as a class, to get in touch with my mood. I will frequently take short walks outside or drop into chapel. It is especially necessary for me to do this at night before going to bed. I find that if I do not spend fifteen minutes unwinding before I go to bed, I bring the day's problems and activities with me and my sleep is restless. I will also take a larger block of time weekly for reflecting on my general mood of the week. I'll do this by spending several hours alone in my room reflecting or by taking a long walk in a park. It is also helpful for me to get away monthly for a day to quiet down and reorientate myself. The main purpose of my being alone and quieting down is to get in touch with my inner self and to see what moods are underlying my actions. If I find that I am not peaceful and loving, I try to allow the Spirit to become present during this silence and to affect my quality of heart. The quieting down at this point turns to prayer. But my goal is first to discover what is happening deep within myself; after this discovery, which often takes a long time, I will relate to the Lord.

I have found two other ways that are helpful for unwinding and becoming more relaxed and in tune with the Spirit. The first is to be alone, quiet, and engage in activities that I enjoy that are not related to my work. This ranges from light reading or spiritual reading to watching a good TV show. I am also helped to relax by some sports events, plays, and concerts. But it is important for me to avoid certain TV shows and movies. I often find that I am not more relaxed after them but more tense; I have just substituted one type of intense mental activity for another. Second, it is helpful for me to do simple chores that don't require much intellectual activity: cleaning my room, doing laundry, watering plants, shopping. All four of these ways of being alone are helpful for me, and I include them as part of my asceticism. I enjoy my work and have a tendency to pursue it all the time; it is often hard to slow down and take a short break from it. But if I don't do it, I lose touch with the quality of heart which reflects the Spirit's influence in my work. In general, I find that if I'm resisting being alone and quiet, there is something wrong that should be dealt with. Normally the peace that follows these quiet breaks is reward enough to keep me doing them. I should add that I have many other ways of getting in touch with myself and of relaxing, such as long talks with a close friend and relaxing in social groups. But I have noticed that the periods of being alone and quiet form the most indispensable rhythm for me and are the most important practice I do in this area.

The negative principle for keeping our minds in touch with the Spirit and not our lower human nature is really closely related to the negative principle for the use of our bodies. We all have the roots of the capital sins within us. These roots can dominate our motivation. They may relate primarily to the physical side of our being, such as gluttony, sloth, and lust, or to the psychological side of our being, such as pride, covetousness, envy, jealousy, and hatred. We must be realistic in acknowledging these roots of sin in ourselves and examine ourselves regularly to make sure that these inclinations are not dominating our motivation, removing us from the influence of the Holy Spirit. Thoughts and imaginings that flow from these tendencies must be recognized and discarded when they occur; occasions of temptation toward these activities must be avoided. This negative principle for the use of our minds to facilitate union with the Spirit relates directly to the positive principle given, since often it is when we are alone that we become aware of our motivation, whether it flows primarily from the Spirit or from the capital sins. We must be wary of under-emphasizing this dimension of asceticism in an unconscious reaction to a previous approach to asceticism in which it was overly prominent.

Directed by the Spirit: Prayer

To provide conditions in which the Spirit can regularly influence our motivation and keep us directed toward doing the Father's will in love and peace, it is not enough only to have rhythms for our bodies and our minds; we must also have a regular pattern of spiritual activities. I list this as an aspect of asceticism because, like the first two dimensions, it demands a good deal of time in our day, time that is not readily available and time from activities that are often less demanding and more immediately enjoyable. The practical question in this area is: What rhythm of spiritual activities is necessary to keep us directed by the Spirit in knowing and doing the Father's will in love? Three daily rhythms are important for myself: prayer, consciousness examen, and writing in my spiritual journal.

It is perhaps unnecessary to discuss prayer as a rhythm for keeping in tune with the Spirit. All Christian tradition confirms the fact that the most zealous servants of the Lord treasured prayer and built times into their schedules for it, no matter how busy they were. This prayer has three dimensions: personal prayer alone, shared prayer in a group, and liturgical prayer. For me thirty minutes of daily personal prayer is important. I pray in the morning, and it often happens that I leave prayer with an entirely different attitude toward serving the Lord during the day because of our union during this prayer. Shared prayer is also becoming more important for me. I am discovering the value of being in the midst of a community very simply expressing their relationship to the Lord. I find myself buoyed up by the community's faith and often through their witness more sensitive to areas of my life where the Lord has been working unrecognized. Finally, it is necessary for me to celebrate the Eucharist regularly, both to preside as the celebrant and to attend and feel part of the community. The Eucharist and personal prayer have always been recognized as central to a life of faith. I believe that I am discovering, along with many others, that some form of regular shared prayer in a group is also an important element in keeping in tune with the Spirit.

Consciousness Examen

A second important rhythm for maintaining a quality of heart during my activities that reflects the presence of the Spirit is regular consciousness examen.[2] Most of our day is spent in activity; consequently, it is important to examine this activity regularly to see whether it is truly directed toward the love and service of God. Since the quality of our external activity is determined by our inner moods, it is important to examine these moods to see if they flow from the Spirit's presence; individual actions will be expressions of this quality of heart. I prefer to call this an examination of "consciousness" and not simply an examination of "conscience," since the examination is concerned primarily with the quality of our heart that underlies our actions, rather than with the individual actions themselves. We are by now familiar with the signs of the Spirit's presence: peace, patience, love, joy. We must apply these criteria to the main actions of our day. Reviewing each of our major activities, we ask ourselves whether we performed them with a real desire to love and serve the Lord and others; this desire is usually accompanied by peace, patience, love and joy. If this was our underlying motivation and quality of heart, we can be assured that we have been responding to the

Spirit's presence in our activities. To the degree that this was not our quality of heart, we have not been acting under the influence of the Spirit. I make a fifteen minute consciousness examen around noon to reflect on my morning and reorientate myself for the afternoon. I also make shorter examens in the morning right after I get up and in the evening before going to bed.

There is a very simple method for making this examen consisting of five steps. I will describe a typical noon examen taking about fifteen minutes, though it may be shorter or longer depending on time available and personal need. The first step is quieting down and beginning with an opening prayer to the Spirit. The examen is a prayer and so it must be done under the influence of the Spirit to be effective. We ask the Spirit to enlighten us so we can recognize where God has been present and absent in our morning. Examen as a prayer is different from daily meditation since it has this specific purpose. The second step is thanking God for the blessings of the morning. If we are in tune with the Spirit, we will become more conscious of how God has been present and active both in and around us. We begin our examen, then, by first thanking God for his blessings. I find that I am often unaware of how God has been present until I explicitly reflect on this during examen.

Third, we review the quality of heart that underlay our specific actions of the morning to see if it reflected the presence of the Spirit. This review has two parts. First, we systematically look over all the actions of the morning to see whether we have performed them with a real desire to love and serve the Lord, or whether we have performed them for some lesser motive. I find it best to take the main events chronologically. I often find that my desire to serve the Lord has been drowned out by some particular problem, and that I have spent the morning with little or no desire to love and serve him in my actions. I am not aware of this until I explicitly stop to reflect on it at noon. The second part of the examen is called the particular examen. During this part we review some pattern in our life that has been the dominant obstacle to the Spirit and see whether it has been an obstacle that morning. For myself this could mean reviewing my attitudes to a person I dislike or toward classes with which I am discouraged. I review the morning to see if I have been acting in resentment toward the person or discouragement toward the class. It is helpful to

keep the same particular examen as long as the situation continues to
remain a major obstacle to the Spirit. When the problem recedes, we
choose another area. To do this most effectively it is helpful to have a
particular ejaculation or phrase to substitute for the destructive pattern. For instance, rather than allow myself to cherish resentment toward a person I dislike, I might say: "Jesus, meek and humble of
heart, make my heart like unto thine." I imagine the troublesome situation ahead of time and have the phrase in mind as I envision it. As
the actual situation arises, the phrase begins to come almost automatically to mind.

The fourth step of the consciousness examen is acknowledging
our fault and asking for forgiveness. It is good to experience our sinfulness because until we admit it we do not know how much we need
God's help to transform it. At this time we can rest in the Lord as sin-
ners, but then love him even more because Jesus has given us the potential to be freed from our sinfulness by his grace. The fifth step is
making resolutions for the afternoon. We are now aware of our destructive patterns, and we have asked forgiveness for our faults. It is
helpful to concretely envision the events of the afternoon, especially
the area related to our particular examen. We ask the Lord for grace
so that we will not fall into the sinful patterns, losing contact with the
Spirit.

The examen will differ from day to day. As we quiet down, we
may become aware that the Lord has been active in our life all morning, and we have been responding by performing our actions with
real love and service. We may want to spend the majority of the time
just thanking the Lord for this presence, spending just a minute or
two at the end doing a systematic review of our actions followed by
acts of contrition and resolution. Or as we quiet down, we may become aware that we have spent the morning with absolutely no
awareness of serving the Lord and have been impatient and unloving,
especially in a particular situation. We may want to acknowledge
this immediately and rest in sorrow before the Lord, begging for the
grace to be healed from this sinful pattern. There may be little awareness of blessing because of heightened awareness of our sin. The goal
of the examen is to open our hearts to the Lord and let the Spirit
repossess them more deeply. If the quality of our hearts has reflected
the presence of the Spirit, there is little need for detailed examen;

however, if the quality of our hearts has reflected the Spirit's absence, then it is essential to catch ourselves so that we do not allow ourselves to continue to be directed by our lower human nature. Being present to the Lord during the midst of our busiest days will always give us new energy to serve God and one another with even greater peace and joy. This being present, therefore, remains important, even when we are not caught in a pattern of blocking the Spirit. For me the peace and joy that result give the motivation to continue to take time from a busy schedule; it is worth it just to get rid of the anxieties connected with work that block our experience of his presence.

The Spiritual Journal

The third important rhythm for me to stay attuned to the Spirit is keeping a spiritual journal. This rhythm is closely related to the consciousness examen. After I get up, shower, and shave, I sit quietly in my room and jot in my journal; then I make my morning meditation. It is important for me to jot in my journal early in the day for two reasons: first, I am better able to clear my head to focus peacefully on the Lord during morning prayer if I have already processed my moods; second, I look ahead to my day and draw together possible problems and approaches to them so that I will be prepared for them when they arise. Writing in my journal early in the day enhances both my personal prayer and my daily service. My entries will sometimes only take five minutes; other times they may take fifteen minutes. I sit quietly in my chair for a few minutes and then begin to record what bubbles to the surface. I do not try to control what happens. As I become conscious of a dominant mood or feeling, I begin to write. The first goal of this writing is to become aware of my moods. Having become aware of them and written them in a free-floating fashion in my journal, I begin to relate them to the Lord. The process of relating them to the Lord generally arises spontaneously after my moods have been adequately expressed. I do not begin meditation itself until I feel peaceful before the Lord. The matter for meditation often comes from this process. The spiritual journal is an aid toward living with the Spirit that is just being recognized. Since there is no standard traditional format to present at this time, I will now present what I do and how it helps me. I believe that the journal will be used very differently by different people. These remarks should be seen as merely one way to use the journal.

The most common entry in my journal relates to moods of anxiety produced by anticipation of the activities of the coming day. Often I have had dreams during the night in which these moods have been reflected, and I wake up anxious but am not certain exactly why. As I permit myself to experience these moods more fully, they begin to crystallize and attach themselves to particular situations coming up in my day. For instance, if I have a difficult passage to write for a book or an article the coming day, I may be anxious about it during sleep and wake up anxious. As I wait I will gradually be able to attach this anxiety to my worry over writing well and finishing the writing within the amount of time available to me. After I have done this I spontaneously want to reflect on the mood in terms of serving the Lord: Is this particular mood an aid or an obstacle to love and service? A mood of anxiety is usually an obstacle. I then acknowledge this and bring it to the Lord and ask him to replace my destructive anxiety with confidence in him so that I can serve him better. When I have acknowledged the mood and brought it to the Lord for help, I experience a new sense of peace. I am now able to respond more freely to the Spirit during my morning meditation and during my daily activities; for meditation I may choose an image or saying of Jesus that speaks to the mood. If this mood promises to be dominant during the day, I will take it as my particular examen. I will envision the situation in which this anxiety will occur and choose a helpful behavior to put in its place, such as "Sacred Heart of Jesus, I place my trust in thee." I jot both the situation and my desired behavior in the journal. If, as in the above case, it concerns anxiety over writing, I recall it both during my noon and during my evening examens to see how often I have been able to replace my anxiety with this ejaculation.

Often my journal entries concern blessings or problems from the previous day that I haven't fully acknowledged. As I quiet down I may become aware that my mood is peaceful. Very often occurrences from the previous day will bubble to the surface, things I had forgotten because they happened in the midst of a busy day. Frequently they concern a good time with a friend or a particular success I had. As I become aware of these blessings, I spontaneously thank the Lord for them. I usually find myself jotting them down with no reference to the Lord; but after getting them in the journal I become more fully aware of his presence in them and I may use the blessing as the starting point for my meditation. During times when I'm experiencing problems, I find it helpful to read parts of the journal in which I was experiencing happiness and blessings. Likewise, as I quiet down I may discover that my mood is anxious, determined by an unresolved problem from the previous day. Again I let the problem bubble up and I describe it in my journal. As I begin focusing on it, I see it in a different context, as an aid or an obstacle to the Spirit. If it is an ongoing problem and seems to be a major obstacle, I may take it as my particular examen for the day.

Another purpose of the journal is planning my service of the Lord. I look ahead to the coming day, reflecting on how I can most effectively use my time and what particular activities I want to accomplish. I will also look ahead to the coming weeks and months to see if there is some new activity for the Lord I should initiate. Before initiating such an activity, such as taking on a parish lecture series or running for a university committee, I will make a list of all the pros and the cons regarding the decision. I will ask the Lord to guide me toward making the decision according to his will by attaching a feeling of peace to one side or the other. After several days, I make the decision that the feeling of peace seems to indicate. It is my conviction that decisions that bear somewhat significantly on promoting the Lord's kingdom will be indicated to us in this way by the Lord. Another important purpose of the journal is recording my observations on life. This ranges from musing over the complexities of human motivation, including my own, to recording spiritual and theological insights that are gradually becoming clearer to me. Since I am a theologian concerned primarily with spirituality, I frequently express my first theological musings on a topic in my journal and then add to these musings insights as they occur to me during my work and prayer.

My journal contains varieties of entries impossible to categorize. But for me the four main purposes are: first, recording my blessings;

second, discernment of my moods; third, planning my service; fourth, recording my theological and psychological insights on life. To better understand how I am relating to the Lord I regularly reflect on the data of these daily entries. Each weekend I spend several hours with the journal to see the patterns of my week. Often this reflection points out trends I had not observed, especially my destructive moods. I then make a large entry in the journal and reorientate myself for the coming week. I will do the same thing on a monthly basis. I can do this most effectively if I have several hours on both days of a weekend. I will spend the first period simply rereading my journal entries for the time period. I will then spend as much time as is available walking and reflecting on the entries. It is helpful to get out of the city and take a long walk. The following day I will record what has occurred to me during my reflections and again reorientate myself to the Lord's service. I find these periodic reflections a great source of peace. My daily schedule is usually so crowded that I don't have the time to reflect adequately on my life. By building in these rhythms, I compensate for this. It is a part of my asceticism to take the time for this quiet—and sometimes painful—reflection, even when time does not seem to be available. Finally, during my annual retreat I review my entire journal from the previous year. This gives me an awareness of the patterns of sin and blessings in my life that provide the perfect context for making a retreat that will flow from my life and be an authentic renewal of this life. I am especially careful to record in the journal the ways in which the Lord deals with me during the annual retreat. I return to these notes often during the year to see if I have been true to the insights given to me during this privileged time.

Challenge of Asceticism

The goal of asceticism is to provide conditions in our daily life that enable us to live habitually in tune with the Holy Spirit so that we will both know and do the Father's will. The result of doing this is living with a quality of heart that reflects the Spirit's gifts of peace, love, and joy. But our challenge is immense. For many of us this demands a rearranging of life patterns in order to build in times each day for exercise, rest, quiet, prayer, consciousness examen, and writing in a journal. It can be objected that this is impossible because of the demands of our particular vocation: how can a housewife with children at home find time for all this! I believe that this objection must be considered, but it must also be held against the demands of the Gospel. We are called to love and serve the Lord and one another with our whole heart, whole soul, whole mind, and whole body. And we are able to meet this impossible challenge only to the extent that we permit the Spirit of Christ to transform our own bodies, minds, and spirits and to permeate all our actions. It is possible that meeting the challenge of the Gospel will demand a reordering of our daily schedule in order to build in rhythms that provide the conditions for living in tune with the Spirit. This Christian life-style may be quite different from the secular lifestyle of our culture. Perhaps this is what Jesus foresaw in his parables on seeking the kingdom of heaven—the kingdom which, he was careful to point out, is within us.

> The kingdom of heaven is like treasure hidden in a field which someone has found; he hides it again, goes off happy, sells everything he owns and buys the field. Again, the kingdom of heaven is like a merchant looking for fine pearls; when he finds one of great value he goes and sells everything he owns and buys it (Mt. 13:44–46).

REFLECTION QUESTIONS

1. Describe attitudes toward asceticism you have noted in yourself and in others that reflect a predominantly negative attitude toward human nature and especially toward the body.

2. Describe the daily rhythms you find helpful for keeping your body energetic in responding to the Spirit in doing God's will.

3. Describe the daily rhythms you find helpful for keeping your mind quiet and peaceful during your daily activities.

4. Describe the rhythm of spiritual activities that are helpful for keeping your service in tune with the Spirit. Which activities of your previous day were done in tune with the Spirit? Which were not?

5. Summarize your previous understanding of asceticism. Compare and contrast it with the approach presented here.

VI ONE LIFE IN CHRIST: PRAYER AND SERVICE

Many of us share a false assumption about the spiritual life flowing from the quite recent past, namely, that our prayer is holier than our service. The self-in-God model of spirituality we are presenting clearly reveals this to be a false assumption. All good and holy actions flow from our cooperation with the Holy Spirit. The holiest actions of our day are those done most in tune with the Spirit; these may be either prayer or service. In fact, it serves no useful purpose to contrast and oppose the two dimensions of our life because they are so interconnected: we lead but one life all under the Spirit of Christ. The purpose of the final chapter is to highlight the unity of Christian living. We will discuss three fundamental Christian truths: that prayer and service are equally important, that prayer supports service, and that service supports prayer—and is, in addition, a privileged means in itself for union with the Lord. For clarity we will limit the meaning of *prayer* to formal prayer, that is, our times of withdrawal from activity to express our relationship to the Lord. By *service* we mean all the activity we perform outside of prayer time to fulfill God's will in our life; this includes our daily work as well as all other activities done in tune with the Spirit.

Prayer and Service: Equally Important

The tension between the relative importance of prayer and service reoccurs frequently in Christian tradition. It has run its course again during the last thirty years. I myself, as were many of us, was a product of these trends. During the 1950's the tension really did not exist for us. Prayer—and this was understood to mean times specifically set aside from activity—was without question the most important and holiest act of the Christian. This seemed obvious to us because during the 1950's we were still comfortable distinguishing our sacred from our secular actions. Prayer was clearly a sacred action, since it was directly related to God. In the 1950's we were also comfortable separating activities which flowed from our supernatural dimension, grace, from those which flowed from our natural dimension, our nature. Prayer was the act par excellence of our supernatural dimension. Somehow or other our daily service to the Lord outside the time of prayer never participated in the holiness of prayer. The role of the Holy Spirit in transforming all our being and all our action was not brought to the fore; it was never denied, but it was never discussed either.

But during the 1960's the pendulum swung completely to the opposite side of the spectrum. By the end of the decade we were quite comfortable asserting that service in the world was the most important and holiest act of the Christian. And this service was pinpointed to direct action in society for the furtherance of social justice. The best Christian was now no longer the one that prayed the longest but the one that was most involved in transforming the evil structures of society to make them better serve all people fairly. This conviction was nowhere better expressed than in Harvey Cox's book *The Secular City*. This handbook for the times was devoted to showing how the Bible clearly presents action in history for the sake of the kingdom of God as the most important activity of believers in both the Old and New Testaments. The entire book contained but one or two paragraphs on the role of personal prayer in the Christian's life. With no discussion of the relationship between prayer and service, the assumption was that prayer was unnecessary. I recall reducing the time I was spending in prayer and even feeling guilty and out of touch with the times by preserving personal prayer as a value, even when it meant withdrawing from activity to be with the Lord alone. I recall being somewhat apologetic in letting certain people know that I still prayed daily. It was also indicative of the mood of the times that there were virtually no books being published in the field of personal prayer; the market for such books simply did not exist. Thomas Merton's books were the outstanding exceptions. But we still couldn't get beyond our previous conditioning about the value of personal prayer.

Many of us salved our consciences by asserting now that "our work was our prayer" and we used the documents of the Second Vatican Council to support our position. Our favorite document was the *Pastoral Constitution on the Church in the Modern World*. Unfortunately we never integrated this document with the long tradition in Christianity on the value of personal prayer in supporting activity.

But this is not the end of the story. During the 1970's the pendulum began to swing again. This time, fortunately, it remained in the center of the spectrum. We began to witness, and are still witnessing, a revival of interest in the interior life. The most obvious sign of this interest is the multitude of books—including this one—written on Christian spirituality. The most read books of religious writers today all converge on the area of spirituality. Typical topics include mysticism, transcendence, religious experience, Eastern religions, personal prayer, the charismatic movement, and the Holy Spirit. The tremendous growth of the charismatic movement during the 1970's is also eloquent testimony to this spiritual revival. Yet at the same time this is happening, there has been no diminution of interest in the social dimensions of living the Gospel. In fact, the importance of service in the world as an integral part of Christian living is being even more emphasized. Within the Catholic Church it reached the apex of formal hierarchical expression in 1971 at the Synod of Bishops called by Pope Paul VI in Rome. This synod declared that direct action in the world on behalf of justice is a constitutive dimension of living the Gospel. In short, one cannot be called a good Christian if there is not some direct involvement in working for justice in society. We have arrived in the 1980's with a view toward Christian spirituality that is better balanced than any time during the last thirty years; it proclaims the value of both prayer and service, and—as we will see—emphasizes the integral connection between the two.

Moreover, the entire prayer-versus-work debate sounds strange today. We have moved beyond the artificial separations upon which it was based, sacred-versus-secular and natural-versus-supernatural. We better understand today that we are one person, a person possessing different dimensions of activity but dimensions all working together. We understand that when the Holy Spirit joins our spirit, he transforms each level of our being: body, mind, and spirit. And this transformed being, when acting under the Spirit's influence, does all acts for the Lord; there is no true secular realm of activity. Our holiest acts will be those done most completely under the influence of the Spirit, and there is no reason to think that they ought to be limited to times of prayer. The assertion just does not make sense. It is as senseless as asking whether the most important and holiest moments in Jesus' life were the times he left the crowd to go to the mountain to pray or the times he preached, healed, suffered, and died in response to his Father's will. The Holy Spirit moved Christ both to prayer and to activity. Luke notes pointedly in one chapter of his Gospel that "filled with the Holy Spirit, Jesus left the Jordan and was led by the Spirit through the wilderness" (Lk. 4:1) but also a few verses later that after the time in the desert was over "Jesus, with the power of the Spirit in him, returned to Galilee" (Lk. 4:14).

Prayer Supports Service

It is not enough to insist that prayer and service are equally important moments in Christian living, since both are done under the influence of the Spirit. Our tradition teaches us another truth: prayer and service are interconnected, each mutually supporting the other. The dominant Christian wisdom points out the indispensable value of prayer for supporting a life of action for the Lord. Prayer is a privileged moment of union with the Lord. The purpose of prayer is, simply, communion with the Father and Jesus. Our tradition points out that we cannot be united with the Father and Jesus without becoming more like them. This has a direct relationship to the quality of our service outside of prayer; we cannot be united with the God of love in prayer without simultaneously becoming more loving in action. Paul points out that "the love of God has been poured out into our hearts by the Holy Spirit which has been given us" (Rom. 5:5). During all his writing Paul shows that this love directs us equally to God and to one another. The love for each will be equal since it flows from the same source in us, the Holy Spirit. Jesus himself emphasized the unity of the two loves in our lives by insisting that the two great commandments of love of God and love of neighbor were equal. He then gave us the parable of the good Samaritan to show that this love was not merely a feeling but implied active service for our neighbor's needs. John put the whole matter very bluntly:

> Anyone who says "I love God" and hates his brother is a liar, since a man who does not love the brother that he can see cannot love God, whom he has never seen (1 Jn. 4:20).

Personal prayer done away from the crowds is a privileged time for being filled with love for the crowds.

Thomas Merton deals with the relationship between prayer and service in many of his writings. In *No Man Is an Island* he uses the images of a spring and a stream to emphasize the unity of the two.

> Action and contemplation now grow together into one life and one unity. They become two aspects of the same thing. Action is charity looking outward to other men, and contemplation is charity drawn inward to its own divine source. Action is the stream, and contemplation is the spring. The spring remains more important than the stream, for the only thing that really matters is for love to spring up inexhaustibly from the infinite abyss of Christ and of God.[1]

And not only are the two interconnected, but the quality of our action is related to the depth of our prayer.

> There is no contradiction between action and contemplation when Christian apostolic activity is raised to the level of pure charity. On that level, action and contemplation are fused into one entity by the love of God and of our brother in Christ. But the trouble is that if prayer itself is not deep, powerful and pure and filled at all times with the spirit of contemplation, Christian action can never reach this high level.[2]

And for Merton, cloistered contemplative that he was, the highest form of Christian life is not merely praying, but sharing the fruits of prayer in the world.

> Hence I want to say that the highest form of life is this "spiritual life" in which the infinitely "fontal" (source-like) creativity of our

being in Being is somehow attained and becomes in its turn a source of action and creativity in the world around us.[3]

The value of personal prayer in supporting service is expressed well by William James in his classic book, *The Varieties of Religious Experience.* I find his conclusions especially compelling because James does not claim to be writing from his own experience—he had no commitment to protect or defend. He simply bases his conclusions on the reports of the people who claim to be religious. In James' observation of these people, if there is no prayer, there is no valid religion, for prayer is "the very soul and essence of religion." Quoting a French author of his day, he describes what he means by prayer.

> Prayer is religion in act; that is, prayer is real religion. . . . Religion is nothing if it be not the vital act by which the entire mind seeks to save itself by clinging to the principles from which it draws life. This act is prayer, by which term I understand no vain exercise of words, no mere repetition of certain sacred formulae, but the very moment itself of the soul, putting itself in a personal relation of contact with the mysterious power of which it feels the presence—it may be even before it has a name by which to call it. Wherever this interior prayer is lacking, there is no religion; wherever, on the other hand, this prayer rises and stirs the soul, even in the absence of forms or of doctrines, we have living religion.[4]

Having given this understanding of prayer, James moves immediately to show how prayer supports action. He asserts that the contact of the religious person with the power worshiped in prayer awakens energy that cannot be tapped in any other way.

> Through prayer, religion insists, things which cannot be realized in any other manner come about: energy which but for prayer would be bound is by prayer set free and operates in some part . . . of the world of facts.[5]

Thus at all stages of the prayerful life we find the persuasion that in the process of communion energy from on high flows in to meet demand, and becomes operative within the phenomenal world. . . . The fundamental religious point is that in prayer, spiritual energy which otherwise would slumber does become active, and spiritual work of some kind is effected really.[6]

James' observations are based on his study of many world religions, Christianity being one of them. The classic expression of this basic religious truth from within the Christian tradition was made, in my opinion, by Evelyn Underhill in her book *Mysticism*. The book describes the entire range of Christian religious experience, from its beginnings to its culmination. It concludes with the fact not appreciated by most of us: at their highest level of union with God the Christian mystics can be characterized not merely by the quality of their prayer but also by the intensity of their activity for the Lord. The false stereotype of mystics as delicate people hidden away in convents is simply not borne out in history. Underhill states bluntly: "All records of mysticism in the West . . . are also the records of supreme human activity."[7] She calls to our attention the following examples: Teresa of Avila, John of the Cross, Francis of Assisi, Ignatius Loyola, Eckhart, Catherine of Genoa, Vincent de Paul, Bernard of Clairvaux, Catherine of Siena, Joan of Arc, and St. Paul himself. Underhill notes that most of these mystics have, in fact, left the world for a time as a necessary condition of establishing their communion with the Absolute, but this withdrawal was only the first step.

But having established that communion, they re-ordered their inner lives upon transcendent levels—being united with their Source not merely in temporary ecstasies, but in virtue of a permanent condition of the soul, they were impelled to abandon their solitude; and resumed, in some way, their contact with the world in order to become the medium whereby that Life flowed out to other men. To go up alone into the mountain and come back as an ambassador to the world has ever been the method of humanity's best friends. This systole-and-diastole motion of retreat as the preliminary to a return remains the true ideal of Christian mysticism in its highest development.[8]

Underhill echoes James and Merton in pointing out the value of union with God in prayer for supporting activity in the world.

> With the attainment of a new order, the new infusion of vitality, comes a new responsibility, the call to effort and endurance on a new and mighty scale. It is not an act but a state. Fresh life is imparted, by which our lives are made complete; new creative powers are conferred. The self, lifted to the divine order, is to be an agent of the divine fecundity; an energizing center, a parent of transcendental life.[9]

Perhaps a note should be added on the role of Jesus' prayer in supporting his service. It is very difficult to talk about Jesus' formal prayer because it is so intimately related to our theological understanding of the relation between his divine and human natures. But even a superficial glance at the Gospels shows that Jesus' public life was marked by a regular rhythm of both prayer and action and that his prayer seemed directly to support his action. Leaving aside the whole question of the relationship of his hidden life at Nazareth to his subsequent ministry— which could be very significant for our purpose—it is clear that Jesus frequently withdrew to be with his Father alone. He prayed in the morning, during the day, and at night.

> In the morning, long before dawn, he got up and left the house and went off to a lonely place and prayed there (Mk. 1:35).

> Directly after this he made his disciples get into the boat and go on ahead to Bethsaida, while he himself sent the crowd away. After saying goodbye to them he went off into the hills to pray (Mk. 6:45–46).

> Now it was about this time that he went out into the hills to pray; and he spent the whole night in prayer to God (Lk. 6:12).

That Jesus prayed regularly is clear; it is also clear that Jesus spent time in prayer before key moments in his ministry. The Gospels point out that he spent many such extended periods in prayer: before beginning his public life; before giving his first major preaching, the Sermon on the Mount; before choosing the twelve apostles; before leaving Galilee and going down to Jerusalem; and, finally, on that night after the Last Supper in the garden of Gethsemane before his arrest and suffering. It is observed that his prayer seemed to give him both vision to know what his Father wanted of him and added strength to do it.

The relationship of prayer in supporting service is clear from observing both the lives of the mystics and the life of Jesus. I believe that we all have evidence to support this truth from our own lives. I can say that the quality of my service for the Lord is directly related to my faithfulness to personal prayer. Of course, many factors are involved, but I have noticed that when I omit personal prayer, service suffers. There are many reasons why I put off prayer: busyness during special periods of the year, hypertension which makes quiet presence to the Lord difficult, boredom in prayer during periods when the Lord seems absent. But whatever the reason, I find that I cannot omit daily prayer over a number of days without hurting my service. On the other hand, the opposite is true. When I regularly withdraw to spend time with the Lord, especially if the Lord has blessed the time together with the experience of God's presence, I find that I leave prayer and enter activity with an entirely new horizon for the day. Prayer puts me in contact with my deepest self, awakening the Spirit and giving me new energy to serve the Lord, surer directions for decisions to be made, and deeper peace and joy. There are times when I honestly do not have the time to pray because of the demands of my work. But I must be ruthlessly honest with myself, lest I rationalize omitting prayer when I could fit it in. I have often noticed that when I am able to squeeze prayer in, my service is accomplished more efficiently and effectively. I can witness to the truth of Merton's insight: without contact with the spring of love in personal prayer the stream of activity for the Lord dries up.

Service Supports Prayer

Christian tradition has always insisted that regular personal prayer is necessary for effective Christian service. However, it has not adequately insisted on the opposite, that our service supports our prayer. In fact, the best preparation for prayer is a life dedicated to serving the Lord by always doing God's will. This is easy to understand;

if the Holy Spirit has been influencing all our actions, it is easy for the Spirit to influence our prayer: we are already in tune. However, if our service has not been in tune with the Spirit, it becomes much more difficult to pray. Merton goes so far as to say that we will not be able to reach a deep level of union with God in prayer if we are not continually giving ourselves to others in service.

> One of the paradoxes of the mystical life is this: that a man cannot enter into the deepest center of himself and pass through that center into God, unless he is able to pass entirely out of himself and empty himself and give himself to other people in the purity of a selfless love.[10]

One side effect of performing service in union with the Spirit is that spontaneous prayers to the Lord rise up in our hearts all day long. The Lord becomes our companion in all our service; God is present helping us when we are not specifically adverting to God's presence, and God is present and breaks forth into our consciousness at frequent intervals during our service.

We have been understanding *service* as all the activity we do outside times of formal prayer in union with the Spirit in order to fulfill the Lord's will in our lives. Service has many, many dimensions, but perhaps its most important dimension is the conscientious fulfilling of our daily jobs. These jobs must be spiritualized whether we are housewives, businessmen, or priests. Somehow or other we have to relate our often humdrum daily activities to the love and service of the Lord and other people, whether they be our families, friends, clients, customers, or communities. It is easier to see how this is more possible for a housewife than a businessman, but I believe that the principle applies equally to both. The largest part of our day is spent in our work. This work, then, becomes the main context for living in tune with the Spirit. We must find ways to insure that it can be performed with the Spirit in love. In this way our hearts will be moving toward the Lord in our activity and will then easily be able to move to the Lord in prayer. For many of us, the basic asceticism of our lives will be this effort to fulfill God's will by giving ourselves totally to those we serve in one way or another in our daily jobs.

Another dimension of this service being recognized today as an essential part of the Christian life is active involvement in society, working for justice and peace for all members of our community, our nation, and our world. As conscientious Christians we will be open to allow the Spirit to lead us toward the particular involvement appropriate for our state in life. In the past we have been too quick to pass this responsibility to others; today each of us is being called to become involved in some way.

It is not enough to see service simply as a means of supporting personal prayer. Service is a privileged time of union with the Lord, valuable in itself. I believe that our age is experiencing this truth in a new way. As we habitually perform our actions under the influence of the Spirit, the Spirit's activity in us grows. Many Christians report types of peak experiences in their work; at special moments their activity is taken over and performed in a radical way under the influence of the Holy Spirit. These religious experiences are set in everyday life; for some they surpass in intensity their prayer experiences. I believe that I can witness to this phenomenon in three areas of my service. I experience the Spirit's activity as superseding my own most frequently while preaching at Mass. I always prepare the homily and have an outline of the points I want to make. But it has often been my experience that after I start giving it, provided that the Mass to that point has been devout, something happens and I find myself saying things I had not planned. I find myself freed to speak right from my heart directly to the hearts of the listeners, saying just the right things, I am told, for their needs. I know that I am saying more than I planned ahead of time, in a spontaneous and extremely effective way. I believe that at these times the Spirit takes over and works in me, supplanting my more ordinary conscious preaching. At the end of these experiences I feel a great joy and enthusiasm for the Lord.

I believe that I have also had these experiences giving classes and talks on theology. Granted that I have prepared the class or talk and that I am not too anxious about presenting it, I find that I am sometimes freed to draw upon buried knowledge and personal experiences, presenting them in a way that touches my listeners just where they are. It could be objected that I am simply exercising a habit acquired over the years of practice, but this explanation does not do justice to my experience. I experience a qualitative difference during these moments, a reverence and conviction that is not typical of the rest of my presentation. After these moments, usually after class, I am aware that something special has happened, and I spontaneously thank the Lord for helping me serve God more effectively.

A similar thing happens in counseling others. I find that I can be plodding along, trying to listen as best I can and make appropriate responses to help the person get in touch with the problem, when I break into a different mode. I become empathetic and enlightened; I begin asking the right questions and making responses that open the person's understanding of inner experiences in a new way. Again I feel a qualitative difference in myself, a closeness to the Lord and a reverence. I believe that the Spirit's activity has superseded my own.

In all three of these activities the experience happens by itself; I cannot predict it. I am often not even aware that it is happening when it begins. Usually toward the end of the experience I am aware that I am more fully engaged than normal, but it is not until the experience is entirely over that I am fully aware that it has happened. At this point I become more quiet, reverent, deeply conscious of God's work in me, and very grateful. These experiences strengthen me to continue serving the Lord. However, I do not believe that this type of experience during service is reason to abandon personal prayer. I find that these experiences occur more regularly for me when I have been faithful to prayer. It's as though prayer puts me in tune with the Spirit; then I leave prayer and serve God under the influence of the Spirit, and then, for some reason, the Spirit's activity rather dramatically supersedes my own. I often use these experiences the next day as the starting point for my daily meditation. By focusing upon them, the Lord is often able to increase my realization of how present and active God is in my life, and I am able to rest quietly in this presence.

One Life in Christ

The goal of the spiritual life is to allow the Spirit of Christ to influence all our activity, prayer as well as service. Our role in this process is to provide conditions in our lives to enable us to live in tune with his Spirit. Our effort is not a self-conscious striving to fill ourselves with the important Christian virtues; it is more getting out of the way and allowing his Spirit to transform all our activities. Christ will do the rest. His Spirit has joined ours and will never abandon us. Gradually we become more and more sensitive to the movements of Christ's Spirit in our own hearts; simultaneously we grow in sensitivity to the movement of his Spirit in others. Subtly our vision of the world changes. We begin seeing everything in relationship to Christ and the Father, and so we carry on a continual dialogue with them. Without really trying, we find ourselves fulfilling Paul's injunction to the Ephesians to "pray always." It becomes clearer and clearer what Paul was trying to express when he exclaimed to the Galatians that "I live now not with my own life but with the life of Christ who lives in me" (Gal. 2:20). Before his conversion he had not known this power. Now the reality of the new life he had received through the Spirit of Christ so overwhelmed him that it seemed as though everything he treasured flowed from this life, as, indeed, it did. He can only pray for his people that they may receive this same life from the Spirit and so know Christ and his love.

> This, then, is what I pray, kneeling before the Father, from whom every family, whether spiritual or natural, takes its name: Out of his infinite glory, may he give you the power through his Spirit for your hidden self to grow strong, so that Christ may live in your hearts through faith, and then, planted in love and built on love, you will with all the saints have strength to grasp the breadth and the length, the height and the depth; until, knowing the love of Christ, which is beyond all knowledge, you are filled with the utter fullness of God (Eph. 3:14–19).

And so he prays for them, and we pray for one another.

REFLECTION QUESTIONS

1. Give examples from recent days how personal prayer has supported your service and how omitting it has hurt your service.

2. Give examples from recent days of how service, performed in tune with the Spirit, has seemed to make personal prayer easier.

3. Have you had experiences in which your service seems to have been taken over by the Spirit in a special way? Explain.

4. Describe areas of your life in which you are becoming more aware of the Spirit's presence and activity. How do you relate these areas to Galatians 2:20: "I live now not with my own life but with the life of Christ who lives in me"?

5. Describe how your understanding of the role and importance of personal prayer has developed over the years. Compare and contrast it with the understanding presented here.

NOTES

Chapter I: Two Models of Spirituality

1. All New Testament quotations are from *The Jerusalem Bible,* except where otherwise noted.
2. Abraham H. Maslow, *Motivation and Personality,* 2nd ed. (New York: Harper & Row, 1970), pp. 269–270.

Chapter II: Recognizing the Holy Spirit

1. Walter Abbott, ed., *The Documents of Vatican II* (New York: Guild, 1966), "Dogmatic Constitution on the Church," n. 4.
2. *Ibid.,* n. 22.

Chapter III: The Holy Spirit and Personal Prayer

1. Thomas Merton, *Spiritual Direction and Meditation* (Collegeville: Liturgical Press, 1960), p. 79.
2. Merton, *Contemplative Prayer* (New York: Image Books, 1969), p. 41.
3. Merton, *New Seeds of Contemplation* (New York: New Directions, 1961), p. 5.
4. Merton, *Contemplation in a World of Action* (Garden City: Doubleday, 1971), p. 341.
5. Merton, *Life and Holiness* (Garden City: Image, 1962), p. 57.
6. Merton, "On Prayer," unpublished sermon given in Darjeeling, India, November 1968.
7. Merton, *The Seven Storey Mountain* (Garden City: Image, 1970), p. 140.

8. Merton, *Contemplative Prayer*, p. 39.
9. Merton, *Spiritual Direction and Meditation*, p. 67.
10. *Ibid.*, pp. 61–62.
11. Merton, *Contemplative Prayer*, p. 67.
12. Merton, *New Seeds of Contemplation*, pp. 2–3.
13. Merton, *No Man Is an Island* (Garden City: Image, 1967), p. 137.
14. Merton, *Contemplative Prayer*, p. 67.
15. Merton, *New Seeds of Contemplation*, pp. 35–36.
16. *Ibid.*, p. 37
17. *Ibid.*, p. 40.
18. Merton, *The New Man*, (New York: Mentor-Omega, 1963), p. 75.
19. Merton, "Prayer and Conscience," ed. by Naomi Burton, *Sisters Today*, April 1971, p. 410.
20. David Steindl-Rast, "Recollections of Thomas Merton's Last Days in the West," *Monastic Studies*, Vol. 7, pp. 1–10.
21. Merton, *Contemplative Prayer*, p. 42.
22. *Ibid.*
23. *Ibid.*, p. 29.
24. Merton, *New Seeds of Contemplation*, p. 243.
25. *Ibid.*

Chapter V: Guidelines for Living in the Spirit

1. Thomas Merton, *New Seeds of Contemplation* (New York: New Directions, 1961), p. 140.
2. For a fuller explanation of the consciousness examen see George A. Aschenbrenner, S.J., "Consciousness Examen," *Review for Religious*, Vol. 31, No. 1, pp. 14–21.

Chapter VI: One Life in Christ: Prayer and Service

1. Thomas Merton, *No Man Is an Island* (New York: Doubleday Image, 1955), p. 65.
2. Merton, *Contemplative Prayer* (New York: Doubleday Image, 1969), p. 115

3. Merton, *Faith and Violence* (Notre Dame: University of Notre Dame Press, 1968), p. 115.

4. William James, *Varieties of Religious Experiences* (New York: Mentor Books, 1958), p. 352.

5. *Ibid.*, p. 353.

6. *Ibid.*, p. 361.

7. Evelyn Underhill, *Mysticism* (New York: E. P. Dutton, 1961), p. 173.

8. *Ibid.*

9. *Ibid.*, p. 428.

10. Merton, *New Seeds of Contemplation* (New York: New Directions, 1961), p. 64.